Baptized into
the Lord Jesus Christ

Also by the Author:

The First Five Words

If the Bible Taught the Trinity, I'd Believe It

Conscious

Attainable Perfection

8 Reasons Christians Shouldn't Drink

BAPTIZED

INTO THE

LORD

JESUS

CHRIST

MICHAEL W. H.
HOLCOMB

BIBLEDAYS
MINISTRIES

BAPTIZED INTO THE LORD JESUS CHRIST

Published by BibleDays Ministries
PO Box 2515
Williamsport, PA 17703

ISBN: 978-0-9837858-7-3

Printed in the United States of America by instantpublier.com

All quotes from the Bible are taken from the King James Version.

The author uses an upper style for religious writing, capitalizing the eternal places, nouns and pronouns that refer to God, the word Church (when it denotes the world-wide body of believers), and other biblical terminology.

Dedicated to the perception that an overwhelming Christian awakening is about to take place in North America and in Europe. To all those who are cooperating with the Holy Spirit to bring this about, I speak to you blessings and power in the matchless name of Jesus.

———————

A special thanks to:

Jacque Myers,
for the work she put into this book.

Harry Ulmer,
for those important tips.

TABLE OF CONTENTS

MOTIVE AND USE OF THIS BOOK

Beyond the Facts

Though it is steadily being accepted and reintroduced into the Church at large, baptism in Jesus' name continues to be a practice which comes under fire of high profile ecclesiastical figures. It would have been very easy for me, then, to join the chorus of apostolic adherents and simply write defending its validity; but I sensed that God wanted me to do much more than that.

Going beyond an argument for mode and manner, *Baptized into the Lord Jesus Christ* is meant to be a source of encouragement to your faith. I have included over 250 verses in the main text that have been to me a wealth of revelation concerning the baptism that was first practiced by believers. I am sure you will find them to be just as useful.

God wants you to know *why* you are doing what you are doing at baptism. He wants you to see that the exercise of Christian immersion in water is more than a respected ritual; and why it is to be carried out in Jesus' name. As you are about to find out, the implication of water baptism is something which defines and builds your entire Christian walk. It is power.

My prayer is that this book will prove to be a stretching to you as much as anything else, so much so that in future days you will have greater confidence in leading others to the Lord Jesus Christ.

The Study Tools

Besides the regular text, I have included features in this book to enhance and compliment your reading experience.

CHECK POINTS

Each chapter is divided into sections, and after each section is a list of verses which serves two purposes. First, these check points "proof text" or confirm the statements I will have just made. Second, they also add valuable and further insight to the related section. Simply put, check points should be read over carefully, not only to verify but also to discover.

APPLICATIONS

Chapters are completed with a short series of questions. No, these are not review tests, but they are meant to get you thinking beyond the material covered. More than anything else, I want you to see the practical things of baptism.

APPENDICES

I have included in this book some important themes related to baptism yet avenues of discussion that I did not think should be part of the main body of text. These are added in the back as "Advanced Readings" and each one compliments a particular chapter.

YOUR NOTES

Be aware that in the very back of this book are special pages for taking notes.

Finally, I want to encourage you to memorize as many of the following passages as possible, for as you do they will become part of you! You will find that by getting these scriptures in your mind, the Holy Ghost will witness them inside of you. I believe that for many of you, verses you have been reading for years will suddenly "click" and open up with original meaning.

God bless you,

Michael W. H. Holcomb
Williamsport, PA

CHAPTER 1

JESUS CALLS YOU TO BE WATER BAPTIZED

"Jesus made and baptized more disciples than John." - John 4:1b

The Meaning of Baptism

In Acts 19:3, Paul met certain men in the upper coasts of Ephesus and wanted to know who they were. He asked them, "Unto what then were ye baptized?" They responded, "Unto John's baptism." This is all Paul needed to hear. He immediately knew who these men followed and what they believed and practiced, *all because of their baptism*.

When Paul comments on the children of Israel who wandered in the Wilderness of Sin[1] and says they "were all baptized unto Moses in the cloud and in the sea,"[2] Paul was showing that the children of Israel became followers of Moses, *all by being baptized*.[3]

In John 4:1-2,[4] Jesus left a certain place because He knew the Pharisees had heard that He made more disciples than John. How did the Pharisees know Jesus was making more disciples than John? The record shows, *it was all because of baptism*.

Smith's Bible Dictionary has this to say about baptism,

> "Baptism was instituted as an initiation rite of his religion by the Lord Jesus Christ ... to be baptized for Christ, <u>shows an intention to become a true follower of Christ.</u>" – William Smith, Sir. *Bible Reference Library Series* (1987). Westwood, NJ: Barbour and Company, Inc. *Baptism*, p. 32

To all the believers in the Early Church Era, a man's discipleship and his baptism were intricately connected. That is still true. You see, Jesus of Nazareth is looking for more than a group of sympathizers; He is gathering an army of disciples, zealots, converts—people who are sold out to Him and His purposes. Without shame or silence about this objective, He actually makes discipleship to Him the underpinning which supports so many of His promises.

Water baptism is one of the three things in earth that bears witness to Jesus Christ,[5] and biblically speaking, you cannot separate baptism from Jesus Himself. It is all about Him. For you, realizing this significance means making a deliberate and meaningful choice for Jesus Christ—and you *do* want to know what you are doing at the water.

CHECK POINT: MEMBER

1. Jesus openly stated that He was drawing people to <u>Himself</u>.
   - *John 3:32*

2. He said that *the Father* was drawing people to <u>Him</u>.
   - *John 6:44*

3. As many as are baptized into Christ put on <u>Christ</u>.
   - *Galatians 3:27*

4. Baptism <u>into Jesus Christ</u> identifies us with <u>Jesus'</u> death and resurrection.

    - *Romans 6:3-4*

5. It is <u>Jesus</u> who is standing at the door [of your heart] and knocking.

    - *Revelation 3:20*

6. Calling Himself the Bread of Life, Jesus said that whoever would come to <u>Him</u> would never hunger or thirst.

    - *John 6:35*

7. He maintained that the condition for one to do God's will, for eternal life, and for receiving the Holy Spirit was to believe on <u>Him</u>.

    - *John 6:40; 7:37-39*

8. He said everyone was to come to <u>Him</u> and learn of <u>Him</u>.

    - *Matthew 11:28-29*

The Gathering of the People

This quest by Jesus for recruitment is *exactly what the Father intended,* for God willed it that Christ be the leader of mankind. Yes, we need a leader; someone who we can trust, someone who will give us concrete direction and firm solutions, and someone who brings order through the principles of truth. We need someone who is the perfect role model and our ultimate inspiration. Jesus is that individual.

As the Son of Man, Jesus has the power and the right to gather people to Himself for global worship of the one, true God. Eliminating social, racial, cultural, and even language barriers, this Great One from Bethlehem[6] has become the Kingdom's mobilizing dynamic. He is the distinct voice of God for all people and for all time, capable of bringing a unity as no other governing force could ever do.

Jesus is more than a messenger who announces the way to God; He *is* the way to God! Your baptism, your recruitment, then, is an absorption into His permission and destiny for universal organization. He who leads you, leads the world!

CHECK POINT: THE CAPTAIN

1. It was prophesied that one called Shiloh[7] would come, and that "unto him" would the "gathering of the people <u>be</u>."
    *   *Genesis 49:10*

2. It was prophesied that the Root of Jesse[8] would be an ensign—<u>a rallying point</u>—for both the Jew and the Gentile.
    *   *Isaiah 11:10, 12b*

3. It was prophesied that David[9] would be a <u>witness and a commander</u> to the people, and <u>the one shepherd</u> who would feed the people of God.
    *   *Isaiah 55:3b-4; Ezekiel 34:23*

4. God said He would give the heathen (even those in the remotest parts of the earth) for the <u>Son's</u> inheritance and possession …
    *   *Psalms 2:8*

5. … and God will cause <u>Him</u> to establish the world.
    *   *Isaiah 49:8*

All or Nothing

My favorite dictionary definition of *to convert* reads like this:

"To turn to another or a particular use or purpose; divert from the original or intended use." [10]

In being baptized, we declare to God that we will "divert" from our selfish, sinful lifestyle and "turn to" a life dedicated to the righteous purposes and uses of Jesus Christ. This is real belief, real faith; the type that is made alive by pro-active performance;[11] the type that pleases God. It is our *conversion*, our *switch*, our *transfer* to Jesus—not lip service or partial adherence—that unlocks the spiritual promises in our lives.

No, discipleship is not an option reserved for pious personalities. While Jesus died for our sins and has brought a way of forgiveness to us, the worldwide invitation to become a Christian is by no means a backstage pass to Heaven or a gift card which offers freedom from obedience, discipline, or cost to self.

The Bible says,

"Except ye be converted, and become as little children, ye shall not enter into the kingdom of heaven." – Matthew 18:3

"He that wavereth[12] is like a wave of the sea driven with the wind and tossed. For let not that man think that he shall receive <u>any thing</u> of the Lord." – James 1:6b-7

Your discipleship, your baptism, then, is much more than an "outward sign of an inward work," or a ceremony for church membership. You are deliberately entering into a contract with God through the Lord Jesus Christ which, by the way, assumes your loyalty, duty, and passion as part of the bargain.

God is an all or nothing God and completely uninterested in a part-time or temporary workforce. All positions in His Kingdom are full time only. The good news is He is hiring *right now.*

Everything in the Kingdom operates by faith. When you do not have faith, you do not please God;[13] but when you have faith in what you are doing before the Lord and you put confidence in His Word, God will release His power. Therefore, if you believe the water is more than symbolism and more than a little initiation rite that you have to observe for tradition's sake, if you believe it is your conversion to the Lord Jesus Christ, then God will recognize and bless your baptism as being your official declaration of dedication to His Kingdom and to His Leader.

You have to believe you are selling out to Jesus.

CHECK POINT: SOLD OUT

1. Baptism itself is considered the circumcision or cutting of Christ.
    * *Colossians 2:11-12*

2. To be Jesus' disciple, we must deny ourselves, forsake all other priorities, and follow Him.
    * *Matthew 16:24; Luke 14:33*

3. Jesus said if we love anyone or anything more than Him, we are <u>unworthy of Him</u>.

   - *Matthew 10:37-39*

4. He said if we begin following <u>Him</u> but then look back, we are unfit for the Kingdom.

   - *Luke 9:61-62*

5. He said if we would follow <u>Him</u> we would walk in light and not darkness.

   - *John 8:12*

APPLICATION

A. The word "Christian" means "Christ like." Christians are then converts of whom?

B. Jesus was looking for you before you were ever looking for Him. What does that indicate?

C. Since Jesus is calling you, what should you do?

D. Is Jesus is the Leader over the entire world or just over Christians?

E. Jesus requires you to make an entire lifestyle switch, meaning that you follow His teachings, His lifestyle, and His relationship to God: true or false?

F. Is positive notice of Jesus enough? Do you have to become a full fledged convert to be considered a Christian?

G. When does serving Jesus take second priority in your life?

Answers on page 137

Advanced Reading: "Appendix 1: Infant Conversion?" page 103

CHAPTER 2

JESUS IS YOUR SALVATION

" ... there is no God else beside me; a just God and a Saviour; there is none beside me. Look unto me, and be ye saved, all the ends of the earth." – Isaiah 45:21-22

It's All in the Name

It was not, and is not, uncommon for Jews to name children after an action or a condition, such as Ichabod, which means "the glory has departed," or Joseph, which is interpreted "let Him add." In English, we do something similar, except we use nouns instead of verbs: Melody, Joy, Faith, Violet. Our nicknames are even more vivid: Red (for a red head); Chubby; Ol' Blue; Slim. I knew a man called Goat, because of the style of his beard. American Indians named their people with nouns and adjectives, too: Sitting Bull, White Cloud, Little Feet, etc.

Whether in the Hebrew, the English, or any other language, names are always meant *to bring a picture or an idea to the mind*.

The Hebrew word for Jesus, *yeshuwah*, means "salvation."[1] In the time of Christ, this fairly common Jewish name declared *the occurrence* or *the result* of deliverance, health, and help. The simplest way to understand this in the fullness of its Hebrew meaning is to realize that when we say *Jesus* of Nazareth we are talking about *Salvation* of Nazareth.

Let me put it another way. When the angel appeared to Joseph, he spoke in Hebrew (for this was one of the main languages spoken among the Jews[2]) and said of Mary, "She shall bring forth a son, and thou shalt call his name [SALVATION] for he shall save his people from their sins."[3]

Do you see the connection? Jesus came to *do* something, to *give* something; and that something was to save the lost, so His name was called Salvation (*Yeshuwah,* Jesus). People, to whom Christ ministered, addressed Jesus by not just a label of identification, but also by what He was bringing to them: SALVATION!

When we understand the name of Jesus through the Hebrew, we pick up things like blind Bartimaeus calling out, "SALVATION, thou son of David! Have mercy on me!"[4] At Gergesenes, the demons cried, "What have we to do with thee, SALVATION, thou Son of God?"[5] The sign on the cross proclaimed, "THIS IS SALVATION KING OF THE JEWS."[6]

No wonder that when the Apostles preached, performed miracles, or baptized anyone, they did so in the name of Jesus. Salvation to them was not a theological term or expression. Salvation was *the Man* who was Savior; for, in fact, it was—it is—*His very name!*

CHECK POINT: SAVIOR

1. Jesus IS the covenant of the people.
   * *Isaiah 42:6; Matthew 26:28*

2. <u>He</u> has power on earth to forgive sin.
   - *Matthew 9:6*

3. <u>He</u> bore our sins.
   - *Isaiah 53:12*

4. <u>His blood</u> purges our conscience from dead works and all sin ...
   - *Hebrews 9:14; 1 John 1:7*

5. ... and <u>His</u> blood was <u>the blood of God</u>.
   - *Acts 20:28*

6. <u>His flesh</u> reconciles us to God.
   - *Colossians 1:21-22*

7. <u>His soul</u> was made an offering for sin, that we might be made the righteousness of God <u>in Him</u>.
   - *Isaiah 53:10; 2 Corinthians 5:21*

8. <u>He</u> entered into heaven to appear before God for us.
   - *Hebrews 9:24*

9. With <u>Him</u>, we are made alive (quickened) from sins.
   - *Ephesians 2:5*

10. Our sins are forgiven for <u>His</u> name's sake.
    - *1 John 2:12*

Jesus is called ...

11. ... the Lamb of God.
    - *John 1:29*

12. ... the passover.
    - *1 Corinthians 5:7*

13. ... the ransom.
    - *1 Timothy 2:6*

14. ... the captain of our salvation.
    - *Hebrews 2:10*

15. ... the propitiation for our sins.
    - *1 John 2:2*

16. ... eternal life.
    - *1 John 5:20*

17. ... the redeemer.
    - *Isaiah 59:20*

18. ... savior of the world.
    - *I John 4:14*

19. ... God our savior
    - *1 Timothy 2:3*

20. In order to be saved, the Bible tells us that we must confess <u>Jesus</u>.
    - *Matthew 10:32-33*

Baptized Into Him

I have often said that the Kingdom is not about an "it," the Kingdom is about a "He;" and the Gospel is not about ritual, it's about relationship. What do I mean by that? Just this: God did not provide a procedure, a currency, a theory, or an academic course to the world; God provided a Man, the Lord Jesus Christ. This is why Jesus is not only the Messenger of the Covenant; He *IS* the covenant.

Jesus is the revelation of salvation.

Stop thinking of your salvation as a date to which you can point, a prayer you prayed, or feelings you experienced. Your salvation is your connection with Jesus and His connection with you. You need to know that when you ask Jesus Christ to take over your life, He comes and *does* what He *is*: He saves. Jesus embodies the complete means and meaning that God has set up to reach us.

Certainly, your conversion to Jesus of Nazareth begins by you accepting His sacrifice on your behalf. At the cross, Jesus paid for your sins, your salvation, and your soul with His blood; and now you are going to commit your life to Him, which is exactly why water baptism is the complete immersion of your physical body. *All of you* is covered by God's Redeemer, the Lord Jesus Christ. No matter how bad, wicked, dark, evil, and twisted, you are to have no more ownership of your sins.

That means you can no longer deal with your wrong actions in your own way. Furthermore, you are prohibited from both self-punishment and self-pity; and your identity and commitment to particular sins are to be regarded as void and canceled out (thankfully, this even includes witchcraft, cursing God, or selling your soul to Satan).

What I am talking about is clean repentance: You giving up all your sins, and this includes dealing with any real and current obligations that have resulted because of your sin.[7] Your conversion means associating yourself with the holiness and righteousness of God's Son.

Yes, you *can* be totally clean! You *can* be absolutely free! You *can* be completely reconnected to God, and it's all in Jesus!

CHECK POINT: PERSONIFY

1. Baptism into <u>Jesus</u> destroys the body of sin.
   - *Romans 6:6*

2. In <u>Jesus' name</u> forgiveness of sins was witnessed by the prophets.
   - *Acts 10:43*

3. Whoever calls on <u>the name of Jesus</u> shall be saved.
   - *Acts 2:21; Romans 10:13*

4. The Law was our schoolmaster to bring us <u>to Christ</u>.
   - *Galatians 3:24*

5. <u>Jesus Christ</u> is in us.
   - *2 Corinthians 13:5*

6. We are taught <u>by Christ</u>.
   - *Ephesians 4:20-21*

7. We are heirs of God, and joint-heirs <u>with Christ</u>.
   - *Romans 8:17a*

8. Paul prayed that <u>the name of the Lord Jesus Christ</u> would be glorified in the saints.
   - *2 Thessalonians 1:11-12*

9. We are called to obtain the glory of our <u>Lord Jesus Christ</u>.
   - *2 Thessalonians 2:14*

10. We can be saved in no other name than <u>the name of Jesus</u>.
    - *Acts 4:12*

Your Only Hope

God has no side door, no shortcut, and no plan "B" beside Jesus. There is no other Begotten Son, no other mediator, no other patron, and no other prophet through whom the Father has willed to move or speak. There is only one way you and I are going to be cleansed of our sins and stay cleansed of our sins, and that is through the Lord Jesus Christ.

I once picked up a book by a prominent author and televangelist at a Christian book store. I was taken aback when I read his claim that when someone backslides and stops believing in Jesus, they are still saved because of their initial or past faith. In other words, the author was saying that you could *stop* having faith in Jesus and yet still expect God to be gracious to you. I really should not have been as surprised as I was. Faulty theology like that occurs just about every time you take the things of God outside of a relationship realm and put them in a mental or conceptual realm. Obviously, the author had separated in his mind Salvation the Man from salvation the plan.

The same is true when speaking of the love of God. It is very popular these days to present a humanistic slant of divine love by portraying God as an emotional Father who just wants to hug and kiss His human kids and who will approve of them no matter what they do. Again, the error comes because there is a failure to recognize the actual interaction between Christ and man; love, *the attribute,* is made out to be the Gospel message.

The full picture of the Bible shows that Jesus Himself, not a formula, is your guarantee of entering the Kingdom of

God. Your cooperation with the One called SALVATION determines salvation.

Do not fool yourself: the Father takes it very personally when you leave, refuse, or disobey His Son, because it is *all* about relationship. The truth about having faith is, you must *continue* trusting Jesus every day of your life.[8] The truth about God's love is, you must respond *by loving Jesus in return*, and that means fulfilling His commandments.[9] Only as your relationship to Jesus is right can you have absolute confidence of escaping the wrath of God and gaining immortality at the resurrection.

The good news is: SALVATION does not change. He is the same now as always. He is consistent with what He does and in the manner in which He does it. You can trust Him! Furthermore, God *wants* you to be baptized, immersed, and buried into the "Him": Jesus, *Yeshuwah*, Salvation, the Son which is given unto us! By His Spirit, He will help you in the things of Jesus and provide all you need to grow in Christ. The only thing you have to worry about is docking your boat in His port, keeping it tied to His pier; and He will take care of the rest.

CHECK POINT: ASSURANCE

1. The promise of God is in Christ by the Gospel.
   * *Ephesians 3:6*

2. The Gospel is called the testimony of Christ.
   * *1 Corinthians 1:6*

3. It is also called the mystery of Christ.
   * *Colossians 4:3*

4. God considers backsliding as treading <u>Jesus</u> under foot and despising the blood <u>He</u> shed.

   - *Hebrews 10:26-29*

5. If we abide in <u>Jesus</u> we will not sin.

   - *1 John 3:6*

6. We labor for the "meat" of eternal life which <u>Jesus</u> gives.

   - *John 6:27*

7. If we hold "our confidence" to the end, we are made partakers of <u>Christ</u>.

   - *Hebrews 3:14*

APPLICATION

A. What one word defines God's plan of salvation?

B. Are there sins for which Jesus did not die?

C. Jesus dying for your sins says what about you?

D. Jesus dying for your sins says what about God?

E. Do you have to become aware in your spirit/heart that you were saved by Jesus?

F. Because God's covenant is the Man Christ Jesus, what is involved in receiving salvation or "getting saved?"

Answers on page 138

Advanced Reading: "Appendix 2: Does Baptism Save?" page 107

CHAPTER 3

THE WATER AND THE EXALTED NAME

*"... be baptized everyone of you
in the name of Jesus Christ ..."*
– Acts 2:38

Apostolic Baptism

From the very onset of the Lord's earthly ministry, the Apostles baptized on behalf of Jesus.[1] That means that at the time of Jesus' ascension, they had had about three years' experience and were fully aware of Christ's requirements for baptism. So when we read in the Book of Acts that the Apostles exclusively (and without a second thought) immersed the new converts in Jesus' name, we are reading about men who were trained in water baptism *by Jesus Himself.*

CHECK POINT: ORIGINAL

1. Peter commanded everyone to be baptized in Jesus' name.
    - *Acts 2:38; 10:48*

2. Philip baptized in Jesus' name.
    - *Acts 8:16*

3. Paul also baptized in <u>Jesus' name</u>.
   - *Acts 19:4-5*

The Name Above All Names

Being taught by the Lord, the Apostles knew the reason behind using Jesus' name during baptism: it was the exalted name of the New Covenant! They knew that in times past, God had unfolded knowledge of His character and intentions by periodically revealing a new name for Himself.[2] They also knew that since the days of the prophets, God had been setting the stage for another, more complete name to be revealed.

> "And the LORD shall be king over all the earth: in that day shall there be one LORD, and <u>his name one</u>." – Zechariah 14:9

> "And the Gentiles shall see thy righteousness, and all kings thy glory: <u>and thou shalt be called by a new name</u>, which the mouth of the LORD shall name." – Isaiah 62:2

Jesus is the only new, revealed name God produced in the New Testament, which is why Christ, in promoting the use of His name, stated that He had faithfully proclaimed the name of God. True, anyone can say they are of God; yet the Father confirmed Jesus' declaration by showing many signs, wonders, and miracles. Jesus is the singular name that has been presented by God in these last days to define, endorse, and empower everything in the New Covenant. It makes perfect sense that water baptism is to be carried out in Jesus' name.

CHECK POINT: CALL HIM

1. God has exalted <u>Jesus' name</u> above every name.
   - *Philippians 2:9*

2. We are commanded to believe on <u>the name of the Son of God</u>.
   - *1 John 3:23*

3. The Father is glorified when we use <u>Jesus' name</u>.
   - *John 14:13*

4. We are commanded to do everything in <u>Jesus' name</u>.
   - *Colossians 3:17b*

5. Jesus said that He came in <u>His Father's name</u> …
   - *John 5:43*

6. … and that He had revealed <u>the name of God</u>.
   - *John 17:6*

7. Jesus said that He would write on overcomers <u>His "new" name</u>.
   - *Revelation 3:12*

Jesus taught that <u>in His name</u> believers …

8. … have life.
   - *John 20:31*

9. … will receive rewards.
   - *Mark 9:39*

10. ... will work miracles.
    - *Mark 16:17-18; Acts 3:6,16*

11. ... will receive answers to prayer.
    - *John 14:13-14; 15:16; 16:23*

12. Jesus said that when believers gather <u>in His name</u>, He would draw near to them.
    - *Matthew 18:20*

13. Those who believe on <u>Jesus' name</u> receive power to become sons of God.
    - *John 1:12*

The Bible says that <u>in Jesus' name</u>, believers ...

14. ... have power to become the sons of God.
    - *John 1:12*

15. ... shall the Gentiles trust
    - *Matthew 12:21*

16. ... the prophets have spoken.
    - *James 5:10*

17. ... our sins are forgiven.
    - *1 John 2:12*

18. ... we are washed (speaking of conversion and baptism).
    - *1 Corinthians 6:11 with Acts 22:16*

Friend, we have a one-name Gospel; and Jesus' name is the only name upon which the Early Church *was built*, and it is the only name upon which the Present Church *shall be built!*

The Revelation in Matthew 28:19

One of the greatest revelations of the authority God has invested in Jesus' name is found in a statement made by the Lord just before His ascension. Again, Christ had been encouraging the use of His name as the name that would connect man to God. In the following passage, Jesus deliberately ties in His name with water baptism and His divinity.

> "And Jesus came and spake unto them, saying, All power is given unto me in heaven and in earth. Go ye therefore, and teach all nations, baptizing them in the name of the Father, and of the Son, and of the Holy Ghost." – Matthew 28:18-19

Unfortunately, theologians (ancient and recent) have idealized this *one* verse in an attempt to negate the use of Jesus' name in water baptism. Despite the number and clarity of Scriptures testifying otherwise, they have claimed that Jesus was introducing a tri-part baptismal mode distinct from and more correct than the mode used by the Apostles. However, despite this biased and (in all honesty) impetuous interpretation, this exciting passage actually reveals the power of the New Covenant's "new name!"

Notice that Jesus did not say, "Baptize in the <u>name</u> of the Father, in the <u>name</u> of the Son, and in the <u>name</u> of the Holy Ghost," which would suggest a three element baptism. He did not even say, "Baptize in the <u>names</u>." Jesus said what He meant, "Baptize in <u>the name</u>."

Friend, we have but one God. He is our Father; He is a Spirit; and having come in the flesh, He is revealed in the

Son. One God revealing one name: that is as simple as it is, and as simple as we need to keep it.

The context of Matthew 28:19 is, "All power is given unto ME ... THEREFORE." This is the overlooked key for this passage. If you do not get this, you will not get Jesus' meaning. This must get in your spirit! The Father has given to Jesus "*all* power," not just *some* power; and because all power is in the Lord Jesus Christ, "*therefore*" we baptize "*in the name*" of the New Covenant, the only name that operates *as power of attorney for all that God is*, the name of Jesus!

By basing baptismal understanding on the *whole* Bible and not just one verse, we can see that there is actually no contradiction between what Jesus *said* and what the Apostles *did*. The Apostles knew exactly what Jesus meant, and they carried out His orders precisely.

CHECK POINT: ONE PLACE

1. The whole family in heaven and in earth is named by the name our Lord Jesus Christ.
    * *Ephesians 3:14-15; 1:10, 21; Colossians 1:20*

2. Jesus said that all things of the Father were His.
    * *John 16:15*

3. It has pleased the Father that in Jesus should all the fullness of the Godhead dwell.
    * *Colossians 1:19*

Jesus is the only name that ...

4. ... pleases the Father.
    * *Ephesians 5:20*

5.   ... identifies the Son.

     • *Matthew 1:22-23*

6.   ... and brings the Holy Ghost.

     • *John 14:26*

7.   It is the name given by the Father ...

     • *Hebrews 1:4*

8.   ... proclaimed by the Son ...

     • *John 3:18*

9.   ... and witnessed by the Spirit.

     • *Acts 10:43 with 1 Peter 1:10-11*

Friend, when you are baptized in Jesus' name, you are plunged into the depths of God. Therefore, when the devil comes against you, when difficulties arise, or whenever you lift your face to the throne, pull out the "new name" that is over your life, because that is the name which Heaven has given to you and that is the name transfused with all the power of God Almighty: Jesus!

APPLICATION

A. When should Christians use Jesus' name in prayer?

B. What other times are Christians to use His name?

C. Does God exalt other names for Christians to use for healing, for blessing, for help, etc?

D. Isn't Jesus' name only for people who have had special training or who have rarely sinned?

E. Is there a specific pronunciation for Jesus' name?

F. If we want to contact the Father, is there a separate name we use for Him?

G. Is there an exclusive name that can give us an edge with the Holy Spirit?

Answers on page 139

Advanced Reading: "Appendix 3: Jesus' Name is Always Valid" page 111

CHAPTER 4

JESUS: YOUR ONE CONNECTION WITH GOD

"If ye had known me, ye should have known my Father also: and from henceforth ye know him, and have seen him " – John 14:7

The Son Shows the Father

Jesus is the true and the faithful witness to who the Father is. Only Jesus has seen Him, and only Jesus knows His true heart. Jesus' whole ministry was and is dedicated to speaking the things of the Father, showing the things of the Father, and being obedient to the Father. He is God's devoted Son.

Jesus has no hidden agendas of personal ambition that would lead you astray. The only thing He cares about is declaring the Father's will, whether it offends or whether it is welcomed. For this reason, it is impossible for Jesus to have corruption in His ministry because His being is founded on pure and divine righteousness. Jesus has Father's heart. You cannot bribe Jesus, you cannot draw Jesus into a morality scandal, and you cannot tempt Jesus with power. The devil tried these things, but it didn't work. Jesus is the Stone that has been put to the test; and the results show that the Son can withstand any kind of compromising pressure! Jesus has proved that He will sacrifice *everything* for His Father.

Your fellowship with Jesus is your perfect restoration with the Father; and when you are in Jesus, you have perfect revelation of the Father. You can have full assurance that by following Jesus, you will find out *all the truths* of God. Think of it, He who called for Adam, walked with Enoch, appeared to Moses, and instructed Elijah, is now extending to *you* the privileged opportunity of becoming familiar with His supernatural nature. The God and Father who was in the beginning—the Great Creator, the strength and secret of the prophets of old—becomes approachable and contactable through the Son.

You cannot be disappointed by being in Jesus.

CHECK POINT: SOLE SOURCE

1. Only the Son knows and reveals the Father.
    - *Matthew 11:27; John 1:18*

2. The Father is plainly revealed in Jesus.
    - *John 16:25-26*

3. The only way to come to the Father is by Jesus.
    - *John 14:6*

4. Whatever the Father is doing, the Son does.
    - *John 5:19*

5. Jesus speaks the words of the Father.
    - *John 12:49-50*

6. The knowledge of God's glory is seen "in the face of" Jesus Christ.
    - *2 Corinthians 4:6*

7. If you confess that Jesus is the Son of God, God will live in you and you will live in God.

   - *1 John 4:15*

8. Through Jesus we have access by one Spirit unto the Father.

   - *Ephesians 2:18*

The Father Has Glorified the Son

Unlike false prophets who come cheaply professing themselves, Jesus of Nazareth came with a multitude of witnesses! His fulfillment of the prophecies, His virgin birth, His introduction by angels, His confirmation by the Heavenly Voice, His miracles, His wisdom, His resurrection, and His ascension all make up the greatest divine testimony *anyone* has ever received in earth's history! And who is responsible for all this promotion? The Father is.

Pay very close attention to what I am about to say, because this truth is very important to New Testament doctrine: *Jesus is the Word of God made flesh.* I do not have the time here to expound much on this incredible revelation, but let me inform you that God watches over His Word. God is intensely interested that His Word is promoted and that His Word prospers. He has sent His Word into the earth expecting the return of glory given.

"For ever, O LORD, thy word is settled in heaven."
– Psalms 119:89

The Father is not threatened when we exalt Jesus, for He Himself has elevated Jesus, His Word. In His economy, He gets glory through Jesus! Before the foundation of the Earth, He predestined to be ultimately revealed in His Son. The Father wants you to be in the Son; for only when the Son is in you are you in the Father.

CHECK POINT: ON HIGH

1. The Father has made Jesus both Jehovah and Messiah.[1]
   - *John 10:36; Acts 2:36*
2. The Father gives souls to Jesus.
   - *John 6:37, 44-45*
3. The Father knows and honors Jesus.
   - *John 8:54; 10:15*
4. The Father's will is that we see and believe on Jesus.
   - *John 6:29, 40*
5. God commands us to "kiss the Son."
   - *Psalms 2:12*
6. In all things, God is to be glorified through Jesus.
   - *1 Peter 4:11*
7. When we pray in Jesus' name, the Father is glorified.
   - *John 14:13*

Jesus and the Father Are One

The Bible is firm and consistent that there is only one God and that God is one.

"Hear, O Israel: The LORD our God *is* one
LORD:" – Deuteronomy 6:4

"Thus saith the LORD the King of Israel, and his
redeemer the LORD of hosts; I *am* the first, and I
am the last; and beside me *there is* no God." –
Isaiah 44:6b

"For *there is* one God ..." – 1 Timothy 2:5a

That Jesus is the only way to the Father and that the
Father glorifies Jesus means but one thing: Jesus is God!
Jesus does not simply introduce you to the Father and then
step aside. When you meet Jesus, you meet God; for just as
the Father is in the Son, the Son is in the Father!

This manifestation of the one true God is as simple as it is
complex; and it is the great mystery[2] of our Christian fellowship and the great discovery of our baptism into the Lord
Jesus Christ.

Jesus came in the flesh so that God—not man—would
receive all the glory of being Savior. Jesus identified with us
humans and, being God, personally endured our character-
istics of weakness and inferiority. He knows what it is to
think and to live as one of us. He knows all the things we go
through: the birth and the death of life, the highs and the
lows, the good inclinations as well as the temptations. He
understands humanity as well as He does divinity, and that is
exactly why He makes the perfect mediator.

What wisdom, that God would become a man and fulfill
those things that could only be done by man! Christ (or
Messiah) is the office of a man, and yet through Jesus, God
became that man and took that office. Priest, prophet, and

king are also positions of men, yet God became all of these and much, much more in order that He might receive the praise of all creation, by all creation. So if you are in the Son, you are in the glory of the Father, for it is through Christ that God has become everything *and everyone* we need.

CHECK POINT: ON HIGH

1. Jesus announced that <u>He</u> and the Father were <u>one</u>.
   - *John 10:30*

2. Whoever sees <u>Jesus</u>, sees the Father.
   - *John 12:45; 14:7-9*

3. The Father is in <u>Him</u>, and likewise <u>He</u> is in the Father.
   - *John 10:38; 14:10-11*

4. God was in <u>Christ</u>, reconciling the world unto himself.
   - *2 Corinthians 5:19*

5. <u>Christ</u> is the image of the invisible God.
   - *Colossians 1:15*

6. Jesus is called *Emmanuel*, which means "<u>God with us</u>."
   - *Matthew 1:23*

7. God's grace is attributed to Jesus as being <u>His grace</u>.
   - *Acts 15:11; 1 Timothy 1:14*

8. The faith of God is attributed to Jesus as being <u>His faith</u>.
   - *Galatians 2:20; 1 Timothy 3:13*

Jesus is called ...

9. ... the Almighty.
   - *Revelation 1:8*

10. ... the everlasting Father.
     - *Isaiah 9:6*
11. ... God Manifest in the Flesh.
     - *1 Timothy 3:16*
12. ... the Lord from Heaven.
     - *1 Corinthians 15:47*
13. ... and the Only Wise God.
     - *Jude 1:25*

The Bible makes it plain that if you ...

14. ... deny the Son, you deny the Father.
     - *1 John 2:23*
15. ... do not honor the Son, you do not honor the Father!
     - *John 5:23*
16. ... have received Jesus, you have received the Father!
     - *Matthew 10:40; Mark 9:37; John 8:19*

The Anointed One

The Spirit of God is upon Jesus. Another way of saying this is, the Anointing is upon Jesus. He is the Messiah or the Christ, both of which mean "The Anointed One." As the Anointed One, Jesus has the Spirit without measure.[3] All of the Holy Ghost is on Jesus, and therefore the only way that you can receive and partake of God's Spirit is to receive it from Jesus. He is the Baptizer of the Holy Ghost.

Now, let me turn that around and say that whatever gift of the Holy Ghost you receive is only a portion of what belongs to Jesus, which is why, when the Holy Ghost comes to you, He will speak of Jesus.

It is all so interchangeable and inseparable.

Once while I was in South Africa, I was awakened by the presence of God and as soon as my eyes were opened I heard this question loud and clear in my spirit, "How would you like to excite the Holy Ghost?"

I said, "That's what I want to do!"

The Lord responded, "Then you get excited about what excites Him: exalting Jesus."

Let's put it this way: the Anointing points to the Anointed One and then the Anointed One pours out the Anointing.

When you are overcome by the Lord Jesus Christ, supernatural things are released around you. You become open to the spiritual realm and to the interaction of God's forces. You become conditioned for the Holy Spirit to come into you, and that means divine authority and ability. Your focus will change from earthly things around you to the heavenly things of Jesus. For this reason, you who are in and of the Spirit of Christ will have standards, goals, and a lifestyle that many times will make no sense to the unconverted mind.

Are you wondering how you can contact the essence of God? Well, my friend, look no further than He who is Christ! All of the Divine Spirit is flowing right now out of the Man of Calvary; for when you are admitted into Jesus, you will receive an activation of His own spiritual power.

CHECK POINT: ANOINTING

1. The Holy Ghost is called the Spirit of <u>Christ</u>.
    *   *Romans 8:9; 1 Peter 1:11*

2. The Holy Ghost is called the Spirit of <u>God's Son</u>.
   - *Galatians 4:6*

3. John the Baptist identified <u>Jesus</u> as being the One who baptizes mankind with the Holy Ghost.
   - *Matthew 3:11; John 1:29-33*

4. Jesus said that if anyone was thirsty, they had to come to <u>Him</u> to drink of living water, which is the Holy Ghost.
   - *John 7:37-39*

5. When the Holy Ghost is upon us, we know that <u>Jesus</u> abides in us.
   - *1 John 3:24*

6. The Comforter, the Spirit of truth, is sent in <u>Jesus' name</u>.
   - *John 14:26*

7. The Holy Ghost testifies of <u>Jesus</u> ...
   - *John 15:26*

8. ... and glorifies <u>Jesus</u> by showing us <u>His</u> things.
   - *John 16:13-14*

9. The veil of the Holy of Holies was torn in half and opened when <u>Jesus</u> "gave up the ghost."
   - *Mark 15:37-38*

The Heavenly and Earthly Witnesses of Jesus

1 John 5:7 is often quoted in an attempt to prove a divine Trinity, but a look at the surrounding verses proves something else.

Before verse 7, there is the qualifying verse 6 which sets the stage (notice who it is talking about).

"This is he that came by water and blood, even Jesus Christ; not by water only, but by water and blood. <u>And it is the Spirit that beareth witness,</u> because the Spirit is truth."

To what does the Spirit bear witness? to Jesus; that He came by water and blood. Now that John made this statement about the Spirit bearing witness, he continues with this point in verse 7.

"For there are three that bear record in heaven, the Father, the Word, and the Holy Ghost: and these three are one."

In what do these three in heaven bear record? Remember the context. Now verse 8,

"And there are three that bear witness in earth, the Spirit, and the water, and the blood: and these three agree in one."

So, with verse 6 as a platform, it would seem that the real topic here is that the three in heaven as well as the three in earth are actually bearing witness and record to Jesus! Is that the case? Have we misread this? Look at the four verses immediately following to find out,

"If we receive the witness of men, the witness of God is greater: <u>for this is the witness of God which he hath testified of his Son.</u> He that believeth on the

Son of God hath the witness in himself: he that believeth not God hath made him a liar; because he believeth not <u>the record that God gave of his Son</u>. And <u>this is the record, that God hath given to us eternal life, and this life is in his Son</u>. He that hath the Son hath life; *and* he that hath not the Son of God hath not life."

There it is! The entire context focuses on the record and the witness that God has testified of Jesus, that He is the Son of God, and that in Him is eternal life! The Father bears record to this, the Word bears record to this, and the Spirit bears record to this. Similarly, the blood, the Spirit, and— yes!—*the water of Christian baptism,* all bear witness to the Lord Jesus Christ.

CHECK POINT: AMEN

1. Jesus' miracles were actually the Father bearing witness to <u>Jesus</u>.
   - *John 5:36-37*

2. Jesus bears witness of <u>Himself</u>.
   - *John 8:14-18*

3. The Comforter proceeds from the Father to testify of <u>Jesus</u>.
   - *John 15:26*

4. The Scriptures testify of <u>Jesus</u>.
   - *John 5:39*

5. The testimony of <u>Christ</u> is confirmed in us.
   - *1 Corinthians 1:6*

6. God kept the revelation of <u>Jesus</u> hidden from generations since the world began …

- *Romans 16:25-26; Ephesians 3:9*

7. … and it is <u>Jesus</u> who has been manifested in these last times for us.

- *1 Peter 1:19-20; Colossians 1:26*

8. **ALL THE FULNESS OF THE GODHEAD DWELLETH BODILY IN <u>JESUS</u>.**

- *Colossians 2:9*

APPLICATION

A. Should you expect to make real contact with God?

B. How can you make contact with God?

C. Whose confirmation can you count on to support Jesus as being God's Son?

D. Should you be worried about glorifying Jesus too much?

E. When did Jesus become divine?

F. Can you become divine?

G. How do you know that you can still receive the baptism in the Holy Ghost as did the saints in the Book of Acts?

Answers on page 140

CHAPTER 5

ALL THE BLESSINGS ARE IN JESUS

"Lord, to whom shall we go?
thou hast the words of eternal life."
– John 6:68

Your Influential Friend

Have you ever known someone who was able to take you backstage to meet famous people or to show you behind-the-scenes production? Has anyone ever invited you to be their guest at an exclusive event, a luxury spot, or a select operation? If so, you know how special you feel and how much you enjoy the perks of privilege. You also know that while you really do not deserve to be there, you have a legitimate place because of the rank, reputation, and accomplishments of another. In the same way, man does not deserve divine privileges, and yet man *needs* those privileges.

> "Man shall not live by bread alone, but by every word that proceedeth out of the mouth of God." – Matthew 4:4

It is imperative that man has a mediator, a contact, a friend in-the-know. Man needs someone who can appeal to God and secure the authorization of spoken blessings.

Well, my friend, Jesus is that friend!

Keep in mind, however, that you can only go through Him for divine blessings. He is the *sole* liaison who has been estab-lished, authorized, and approved by God. Christ Jesus is God's open-house invitation to all mankind, made available, not by our relentless begging or self-afflicting attempts for pity, but rather by His divine love for the world.

As your one connection with God, the Lord Jesus Christ is the source of every benefit and every answer for which you could ever hope! All has been given to Him by the Father; and when you are baptized in His name, He overflows you with *His* favor and *His* advantages. You obtain inconceivable grace from God; and yet, it is really not *your* grace that you receive but the graciousness of the Father which rests upon Jesus. You enjoy answers from Heaven, and yet it is never *your* credit that gets you noticed but that of Jesus' name which wins recognition.

For this reason, it is so important to be thankful for Jesus everyday. As you know, your sins separated you from God but it was Jesus' intervention that set you up for privilege. Jesus was and is your friend in need, and He is the most important friend you could ever have. He is the only one who knows the ropes, who can pull the strings, and who has the golden key.

CHECK POINT: ADVANTAGE

1. Jesus <u>always pleases</u> the Father.
    - *John 8:29; Isaiah 42:1*
2. Jesus' prayers are <u>always answered</u>.
    - *John 11:41-42*

3. Jesus is the <u>one mediator</u> between God and man.
    - *1 Timothy 2:5*

4. Jesus is our <u>advocate</u>.
    - *1 John 2:1*

5. Jesus is the only one in Heaven <u>interceding</u> for us.
    - *Isaiah 53:12; Romans 8:34*

6. Jesus <u>has the Holy Spirit</u> without measure.
    - *John 3:34*

7. <u>All</u> the promises of God in Jesus Christ "*are* yea, and in him Amen."
    - *2 Corinthians 1:20*

Forget trying to impress God. Jesus is Father's favorite; and the Father is never more pleased than when you cooperate with His only begotten Son. Your faith in Christ and your conversion to Him, make you an honored member of God's family with all the benefits.

Crammed With Benefits

God revealed Himself at the very dawn of time, and throughout the ages continued to show more and more of who He was, until finally, "in these last days,"[1] He sent His Son. You must understand that Jesus is more than a mere "secretary" who lets you into God; Jesus is *the ultimate revelation of God.* That is why the Apostle John called Him "The Word."[2]

If you try searching for any other blessing from or revelation of God outside of the Lord Jesus Christ, you will find yourself in a serious spiritual void. By attempting to use other mediators or methods, what you are saying is, "God, I think you are holding back on me. I think there's more than what you have already given. Jesus is the one who makes a way for me, I know that; but *I want something else*." You will never be satisfied with pure Christianity if you hold to this idea. You will inevitability be drawn away from the Light which God has shown to the earth, into the fatal shadows of deception. There is only one Way *to God* and only one Way *from God*. Nothing is going to be done through any other way, but through the Way that the Father has provided.

Colossians 2:10 says that in Jesus, we are complete. The Greek word in that verse used for "complete" literally means "to cram (like a net is crammed with fish), to level up (like something hollow being filled), to finish (a period or a task)."[3] I like that first definition "to cram," and it says two things to me.

First, every benefit and every provision transported from God to man is *crammed* in the Lord Jesus Christ! Need an answer to prayer? It's in Jesus. Need a divine blessing that will turn your life around? It's in Jesus. Need guidance or instruction from God? It's in Jesus.

There is no reason for you as a believer in the Almighty to assume that your handicapped situations are the will of God. You have a Redeemer who sought you out, who saved you, and who extends to you all the promises of God. Jesus has become your help! And by being on His side, you have the opportunity of having a life crammed with all He has to offer!

Secondly, the reason Jesus can make you complete is because He is complete! As we found out in the last chapter, Jesus does not have partial power; in Him is all power. My grandfather, Rev. Joseph Crandall, preaches it like this, "All means all! If Jesus has all the power, then there isn't any more power!"

Saint of the Most High, do not limit Jesus to just churchy things; He is running everything. Do not think that there are additional blessings or beneficial choices outside of Jesus; He is the exclusive source. Remember, *the Father is the one who sent His Son into the world and gave Him all power,* so it is perfectly legitimate to say that Jesus is your one and only source.

CHECK POINT: ALL IS ALL

1. Christ is all and in all.
    * *Colossians 3:11*

2. All things are of Jesus, through Jesus, and to Jesus.
    * *Romans 11:36*

3. All things are under His feet.
    * *Ephesians 1:22a*

4. All things consist by Him.
    * *Colossians 1:17*

5. All things (in Heaven and in Earth) are gathered together in Christ.
    * *Ephesians 1:10*

6. All things—in heaven, and in earth; visible and invisible —were created by him, and for him.
    * *Colossians 1:16*

7. The Father has given all things into His hand.
    * *John 3:35*

8. In all things, He has preeminence.
   - *Colossians 1:18*

9. If we know the love of Christ we will be filled with all the fullness of God.
   - *Ephesians 3:19*

10. All our needs are supplied according to God's riches in glory by Christ Jesus.
    - *Philippians 4:19*

11. All the treasures of wisdom and knowledge are in Christ.
    - *Colossians 2:2-3*

12. All things are to be done in the name of the Lord Jesus.
    - *Colossians 3:17*

13. All the promises of God are in Jesus.
    - *2 Corinthians 1:19-20*

14. **ALL SPIRITUAL BLESSINGS IN HEAVENLY PLACES ARE IN CHRIST.**
    - *Ephesians 1:3*

Whatever you need from God throw your hands up right now and call on the Lord Jesus Christ! "Him that cometh to me," Jesus said, "I will in no wise cast out."[4]

The Jesus Word Study

I once looked up in the New Testament the phrases "with Jesus," "in Jesus," "by Jesus," and "through Jesus." I then collected these phrases[5] together and was pleasantly surprised at the incredible wealth of revelation listed before me. I would like to share some of those Scriptures with you right now.

Buckle your seat belt and go through the next three pages ready for revelation. If anyone has ever wondered why we should baptize in Jesus' name, this list may very well answer their question.

WITH JESUS

1. We shall appear in glory.
   • *Colossians 3:4*
2. We shall be glorified.
   • *Romans 8:17b*
3. We shall live together.
   • *1 Thessalonians 5:10*
4. We shall reign.
   • *2 Timothy 2:12*

IN JESUS

5. There is no condemnation.
   • *Romans 8:1*
6. The love of God is perfected.
   • *1 John 2:5*
7. Was and is the working of God's mighty power.
   • *Ephesians 1:19-20*
8. God stablisheth us and anoints us.
   • *2 Corinthians 1:21*

9. We are wise.
   - *1 Corinthians 4:10*
10. We are one body.
    - *Romans 12:5*
11. We are chosen from the foundation of the world.
    - *Ephesians 1:4*
12. We are the workmanship of God.
    - *Ephesians 2:10*
13. We triumph.
    - *2 Corinthians 2:14*
14. Is our liberty,
    - *Galatians 2:4*
15. Is salvation unto eternal glory.
    - *2 Timothy 2:10*
16. Is our good conversation.
    - *1 Peter 3:16*
17. Is the simplicity of the Gospel.
    - *2 Corinthians 11:3*
18. Is the prize of the high calling of God.
    - *Philippians 3:14*

BY JESUS

19. Came grace and truth.
    - *John 1:17*
20. Are the fruits of righteousness.
    - *Philippians 1:11*

21. We are predestinated unto the adoption of children.
    * *Ephesians 1:5*

22. We offer up spiritual sacrifices, acceptable to God.
    * *1 Peter 2:5*

THROUGH JESUS

23. Is the resurrection from the dead.
    * *Acts 4:2*

24. We come to God.
    * *Hebrews 7:25*

25. We have trust to God-ward.
    * *2 Corinthians 3:4*

26. We are no more servants but sons, heirs of God.
    * *Galatians 4:7*

27. The blessing of Abraham comes on the Gentiles.
    * *Galatians 3:14*

28. The peace of God shall keep our hearts and minds.
    * *Philippians 4:7*

29. God abundantly shed the Holy Ghost on us.
    * *Titus 3:5-6*

30. God is working in us that which is well pleasing in His sight.
    * *Hebrews 13:21*

Jesus called Himself "the door," but can I tell you that He is more than a one-time entrance. You will always have to use the Door. Jesus the Door will constantly let you out as well as in, so that you can find "pasture,"[6] both spiritual and natural things you need. Jesus is your single entrance to heavenly realms and earthly returns.

Your endless resource is Jesus.

APPLICATION

A. Does Jesus meet specific needs or just general ones?

B. Are there any blessings available to believers that are not in or by Jesus?

C. Are angels or deceased saints commissioned by God to answer prayers?

D. Christian prayer is complex and requires much study and special qualifications to master: true or false?

E. Since all blessings, wisdom, knowledge, etc. are in Jesus, what does this say about Him?

Answers on page 140

Advanced Reading: " Appendix 4: The List" page 115

CHAPTER 6

YOUR IDENTITY IS NOW IN JESUS

"I am crucified with Christ: nevertheless I
live; yet not I, but Christ liveth in me."
– Galatians 2:20

Raymond

I would like to relay a certain story that will best introduce this next subject.

I had prayed several times with Raymond,[1] so had all the altar workers and all the people in Raymond's mid-week home group. He was a prayer-line regular. Putting on that same depressed look, he asked for the same prayer requests: for a physical need (which, he constantly reminded everyone, was serious enough to keep him from a regular job) and for spiritual victory in his life.

One time, I asked him to give me some specifics about his request for victory. I wanted to know why he felt that he was always lacking in this area. At first he beat around the bush but finally he told me. He said that he struggled with wanting to do drugs again and he occasionally lapsed back into drinking. He also confessed that he regularly considered backsliding, "Because," he said, "I just had a really good time when I was out in the world." When he told me that he was fighting lust, I instinctively asked him what he was putting before his eyes. He revealed that he did watch "R" rated movies with nudity and fornication scenes, and he quickly added that he needed victory over this habit as well. He also confessed to having swearing binges and periods of rage. He claimed, however, that he was desperate to overcome these things in his life.

What was disturbing to me about hearing this was Raymond's contradictory yet adamant claim that he was, in fact, a firm Christian. He said that the Lord talked to him all the time, and often he felt that God gave him "words" for people in the church. Raymond also was a strong and proud volunteer at local Christian events. He rubbed shoulders with nationally known Christian figures and had a lot of contacts in other assemblies (ours was not the only church he had attended, believe me). He was also very quick to let one know that he witnessed to the unsaved all the time. "I minister to the ones who the Church despises," is what he would say. Raymond considered himself to be a radical Christian, despite his so-called "personal struggles."

One Sunday he came down the church aisle, searching for someone who would once more pray peace into his soul; but that day, the Holy Ghost prompted me to talk to him. "Something is very wrong with this man," I heard the Lord say. Meeting Raymond up front, I began to interview him, going beyond his usual generalizations and again asking him to be more specific about his problems. He repeated what he had told me before, but the Holy Ghost kept saying, "There's more." I kept probing.

Finally, Raymond pulled the lid off the can: he was angry with God! Raymond's life had not gone as *he* had planned and now he held a grudge against the Lord. "Why can't God just take all this stuff away?" he bitterly demanded. "I know He can! Why doesn't He just do it? I don't have a job, I don't have a woman, and I'm not happy!" I told Raymond that he had no business trying to fit God into his own human will and that he needed to give himself to the Father's will. I said, "If you are baptized into the Lord Jesus Christ, that means that you no longer have rights to yourself. Your identity is now 'hid with Christ.'" Raymond's eyebrows gathered together, his eyes squinted, and he said, "You mean I'm not me? I can't be myself?" I said, "Well, in a way, you cannot be yourself because 'yourself' is sinful. You are supposed to be like Jesus. The Bible says so." With that, Raymond grew very frustrated, not because he misunderstood me; but just the opposite, he saw his heavenly calling *and he did not want to take it.*

Soon after that, Raymond left the church.

* * * * *

As far as my experience goes, Raymond's "me-ism" mindset and lifestyle are epidemic in the Church of North America and Europe. There is a shocking lack of the healthy, sacrificial conformity that denotes original Christianity; but in Jesus' name, that is about to change!

While it may irk the flesh, being converted and baptized into Jesus means switching identities. You are no longer your old self. God has not called you to be a warmed over "you" or to flavor your selfish desires with religious rhetoric and labeling. You have been chosen to adapt to His pattern for living, and that pattern is entirely laid out in the Lord Jesus Christ.

True, you are the building: your stretch of existence, your culture, your habits, your thoughts, your actions, and everything about you becomes the platform on which God is demonstrated. However, your purposes, your dreams, your goals, your expectations, your habits, and your preferences are reduced, *even disposable*, in light of the better will of God. Why? Because you have a new identity, a new family, a new culture, and therefore you have a new loyalty and new obligations.

In becoming a Christian, you make a bargain with God that you will accept and take up another name, another Spirit, and another life—the name, Spirit, and life of Christ Jesus.

CHECK POINT: NEW NATURE

1. Our life is hid with <u>Christ</u> in God.
    - *Colossians 3:3*

2. Our bodies are now the members of <u>Christ</u>.
    - *1 Corinthians 6:15*

3. We are to be found <u>of Christ</u> in peace, without spot, and blameless.
    - *2 Peter 3:14*

4. We are predestinated to be conformed to the image of <u>God's dear Son</u>.
    - *Romans 8:29*

5. <u>Christ</u> is to be formed in us.
    - *Galatians 4:19*

Even Unto Death

Now compare Raymond's idea of Christianity with that reflected in the *Martyr's Oath* (which exploded through the internet some time ago). Made public on January 14, 2007, Dr. Eurgun Caner, President of Liberty Theological Seminary at Liberty University in Lynchburg, Virginia, posted the famous pledge to his blog, "Beyond the Pulpit." Known to be recited in India, Dr. Caner adds that "versions of it have appeared in Persian and Arab countries" and it is even used in Christian wedding ceremonies. More than an impressive recital, this oath is taken by those who are already living it out.

> *Today, I stand as a dead man. I declare that in Jesus Christ, I am saved by His blood and thus I am dead to sin and no longer dead in my sin.*
>
> *Today, I stand and declare that I surrender my will and my life to His will and His life. I shall go where He sends me, without asking questions. I shall go to whomever He sends me, without seeking fame. I shall preach to everyone, even if they hate me. I am an Ambassador of the Cross and must deliver the Message.*
>
> *I shall pour my life out to reach my family, my friends, my neighbors and my city. I embrace the shame of the Cross and I fear nothing but God. I welcome suffering, shame, persecution, beatings, imprisonment and death, but I will not*

be silenced. If I am killed, I pray that my blood should be a harvest for souls.

This is my city. I dare not do less.

Nothing here resembles the quasi-Christianity that Raymond practiced (though he would have quickly claimed that this type of zeal and holiness was identical to his). Raymond was all about Raymond; and Raymond's idea of Jesus was all about Raymond.

Water baptism is the entrance into the being of Jesus Christ, into His salvation, into His inheritance, and, yes, into His suffering and sacrifice. Water baptism is actually the original *Martyr's Oath.*

I realize that there are those who believe that suffering, in and of itself, is a virtue; that they must welcome and even self induce physical pain, hurt, or want in order to gain a revelation of God or to cleanse of the soul. But Jesus never taught such a thing. The kind of suffering that is truly Christian is that which Jesus has already put in motion, an inevitable reaction from the ungodly to the incessant expansion of the Gospel.

Because of His flawless love of God's Word and God's Spirit, Jesus always did and always will offend people. He is the Lamb, but He is equally the Lion. The nature, the mission, and the revelation of Jesus Christ set a Kingdom precedent of aggressive growth and fearless virtue, which will always crosscut sin as well as religious counterfeit. To those who want a soft, sophisticated, sterilized Messiah, Jesus' bluntly replies "Blessed is *he,* whosoever shall not be offended in me,"[2] and then He lets the chips fall where they may.

We who have taken the identity of Jesus are happy to take on the shame and reproach of His cross, for we have been called by Christ to work with Him in a labor that is never to be compromised. People may not like it when we preach and witness, but we are going to keep on preaching and witnessing! People may not like it when they see our righteous lifestyle (a lifestyle that reminds them that there is a God) but we are going to keep on being a godly example anyway! Though we are hated, despised, rejected, or even put to death we know that the same mission that Jesus had is now our mission. His calling is who we are.

CHECK POINT: ENLISTED

1. We are ambassadors for Christ.
   - *2 Corinthians 5:18-20*

2. The world hates Jesus because He exposes sin.
   - *John 3:18-19; 15:21-22*

3. Jesus is the Rock of Offense.
   - *1 Peter 2:5-8*

4. We shall be hated for His name's sake.
   - *Matthew 10:16-22; John 15:18-20*

5. Our sufferings are considered Christ's sufferings ...
   - *1 Peter 4:13; 2 Corinthians 1:5*

6. ... and, indeed, we are called to suffer for Jesus' sake.
   - *Philippians 1:29*

7. We are blessed when we are defamed, persecuted, and falsely accused for the name of Jesus.
   - *Matthew 5:11*

The Resurrection Part of Baptism

Many like Raymond fail to make the connection between *the promises* of God's salvation plan and *the purposes* of God's salvation plan. Raymond was under the impression that Jesus came to help him, and that is all. Yet Jesus came to destroy sin *and* to root the precepts of God in all the earth. Freeing souls from sin *is to that end*, not for making us feel better about ourselves or getting us out of personal jams. Another way of saying this is, you have been saved *from* sin so that you can be saved *for* virtue.

If all you see in Christianity is a welfare program that benefits you, you will not have the power you need in the Kingdom. Like Raymond, you will find yourself frustrated in your faith. Only when you tap into the motive that underlies your salvation can you wield the sword of spiritual authority.

The reason Jesus the Man had influence over the devil is because He was submitted to the will *and commandments* of the Father. Yet Jesus went beyond robotic compliance; He actually delighted Himself in doing the things of the Father. He loved wholesomeness, He loved justice, and He loved the paths of truth. It was this passion for purity that caused Jesus to have no subsequent, illicit activities that would have given Satan an advantage over Him (for the devil has oppressive rights wherever sin exists[3]).

Ultimately, Jesus triumphed over death because sin brings death and Jesus had no sin.

> "Concerning his Son Jesus Christ our Lord, which was ... declared *to be* the Son of God with power, according to the spirit of holiness, by the resurrection from the dead:" – Romans 1:3-4

The will of God is that you be soaked in what interests the Lord Jesus Christ. Yes, you are to be marinated in God's righteousness. The same Spirit that was and is on Him of wanting to fulfill all the will and desires of the Father now belongs upon you.

You are called to be perfectly clean, blameless, and zealous of good works; yet, like Jesus, your calling goes much deeper than merely carrying out some rules. Your righteousness is power, Jesus' power, resurrection power! In being put under baptismal waters, you trade identities, that is, you die with Christ. On the other hand, in coming out of those waters, you rise with Christ and therefore enter into His might and right.

You have the might and right to be above sin. You have the might and right to overcome the world. You have the might and right over Satan because you are a child of God through Jesus Christ. Your baptismal resurrection means that there are no more ties with the old, sinful you and like your Master you are free from the power of the devil!

Let me add another element here. Temptation and trials are a constant part of your growth in Jesus. Therefore, do not be naïve in thinking that maturing in Christ means having less and less feelings of enticement. In fact, the more you grow in the Lord, *the more He will expect you to take.* That's right, *God will entrust you with bigger tests so that you can have bigger victories!*

You would not trust a bridge that had failed to meet certain codes nor would you eat at a restaurant that refused to abide by with USDA regulations. You want to know that things are first tested before you use them.

In school, how do you go from one grade to the next? ultimately, by passing tests. How do you get into college or university? by correctly answering an entrance exam, a test. How do you get into the Olympics? by winning competitions or tests of your skill.

The same thing is true with the children of God. God wants to entrust you with greater authority over sin, the flesh, and the devil; but He first must put you through tests.[4] Cheer up, the Bible tells us that God will help us in every hour of struggle;[5] and in knowing this, your attitude toward the testing of the Lord should not be of hesitation but of welcome.

> "Wherein ye greatly rejoice, though now for a season, if need be, ye are in heaviness through manifold temptations: that the trial of your faith, <u>being much more precious than of gold </u>that perisheth, though it be tried with fire, might be found unto praise and honour and glory at the appearing of Jesus Christ." – 1 Peter 1:6-7

The next time you feel the heat of the fight of faith, remind yourself that because you have risen with Christ in baptism, you are now part of Jesus' own resurrection victory. You will have to ignore the devil because he will tell you all kinds of lies to try to make you quit. Just keep swinging. Jesus won so you will win.

CHECK POINT: LIBERATED

1. <u>Jesus</u> delights to do the will of God.
    * *Psalms 40:8*

2. Jesus loves righteousness and hates wickedness.
    *   *Hebrews 1:8-9*

3. Jesus sits upon the throne to establish and execute truth and justice.
    *   *Isaiah 9:6-7; 42:1-4; Jeremiah 23:5*

4. One of Jesus' titles is The Lord Our Righteousness.
    *   *Jeremiah 23:6*

5. Jesus came to destroy the works of the devil [sin].
    *   *1 John 3:8*

6. Satan has no accusation against Jesus and therefore he has no hold on Jesus.
    *   *John 14:30*

7. Jesus refines and purifies His people.
    *   *Malachi 3:1-3*

8. Jesus gave Himself for us that He might have a people zealous of good works.
    *   *Titus 2:2-3*

9. We are created in Christ Jesus unto good works ...
    *   *Ephesians 2:10*

10. ... to be found of Jesus blameless and without spot.
    *   *2 Peter 3:14*

Real Freedom

While individually they seem like small things, our personal opinions, outlooks, beliefs, and yes our emotions collectively guide our behavior. As a Christian, God has a plan to change your inner workings as well as your behavior.

I have heard people say things like, "I don't want to be a cookie-cutter personality!" What they really mean to say is, "I want to be free to do what I want, when I want, and how I want." Indeed, with such romantic words, they look like the smart and attractive ones—at first.

The heart of sin is the love of self: the belief that you are ultimately right and that you can make everything work by following your own way. However, the problems with such selfish autonomy never come right away. In the end, the world's brand of liberty means freedom to destroy your body, freedom to ruin your soul, freedom to deceive your mind, freedom to corrupt your spirit, and freedom to go to Hell.

Regardless of how much you cringe against being like others, there is a mold, a "cookie-cut," that you must fit into in order to be a Christian. No, it is not enough to simply live better and take up church activity once you are converted. You must see the world through God's eyes, think His thoughts, say His words, and do His works. *Jesus* is the mold into which you are ordained to conform; *and within the expression of Him is true freedom*: freedom from the lies of this world, freedom from its corrupting darkness, freedom from its strangling sins, and freedom from a destiny without God!

Do you know the life that is in Jesus Christ? Do you know what it means to enjoy the benefits of living by truth? Do you know the power of a clear conscience and a clear connection with God? Your conversion to Jesus offers you an open door that you could never afford in the past; if you, like Raymond, do not know what real freedom is like, you can!

Let the world deceive themselves with their so-called independence! Let them mock and ridicule you! You have something they just cannot understand. Do not try to hide your liberty or flinch in the face of adversity. You are baptized in Jesus, now live in Jesus!

CHECK POINT: LIBERATED

1. We are alive unto God through Jesus Christ.
   * *Romans 6:11*

2. We are to have the mind of Christ ...
   * *1 Corinthians 2:16*

3. ... and bring every thought into the obedience of Christ.
   * *2 Corinthians 10:5*

4. We are to put on Christ and walk in Him.
   * *Romans 13:14; Colossians 2:6*

5. We are to abide in Christ Jesus.
   * *John 6:56-57; 1 John 2:28*

6. We are to grow in the knowledge of Jesus Christ.
   * *2 Peter 3:18*

7. We are to grow up into Christ in all things.
   * *Ephesians 4:15*

8. We are to be rooted, built up, and established in Christ Jesus.
   * *Colossians 2:7*

APPLICATION

A. Does a believer have to seek divine assignments for their life, or may he or she assume that God will work with their own desires, plans, and viewpoints?

B. Because God loves you, He would never ask you to put away your talents, your dreams, or the special things for which you have worked hard: true or false?

C. In your own words, explain what the Bible means when it says that we are to be conformed into the image of Jesus Christ?

D. God understands that you have particular weaknesses and therefore gives you some room when you sin: true or false?

E. Does God expect new believers to (A) never change their lifestyle; (B) gradually change their lifestyle; or (C) immediately change their lifestyle?

F. You can be perfectly content in laying aside your will for the will of God: true or false?

Answers on page 141

Advanced Reading: "Appendix 5: Accusations Against Jesus" page 129

CHAPTER 7

JESUS: ACTIVE HEAD OF THE CHURCH

"And in the midst of the seven candlesticks one like unto the Son of man." – Revelation 1:13

Bride of Christ

The definition of "church" is "an assembly" and specifically "a gathering of citizens called out from their homes into some public place."[1] In other words, the Church is not about a building, a hierarchy, or an organization.

Since the beginning of time, the Creator has always had an assembly, a congregation of people—ordinary, yes—but people who went beyond earthly pursuits, obeyed the Heavenly "calling out," and lived their lives for the one, true God. Under the New Covenant, the Church is made up of people from every nation, every tribe, and every tongue that are gathered together under the protection of the Lord Jesus Christ. These called out ones are His project, His constant and beloved work. And regardless of what casual Christianity may be saying today, there is no sideline fellowship beside what Jesus is doing or saying in His Church.

Your conversion is an entrance into God's gathering, and together with all believers, you are called by Jesus' name. You become a citizen and a family member. Therefore, if you are truly of Christ, you will love the Church, love being part of the Church, and love to work with Jesus to strengthen the Church.

Yes, there are quirks, quarrels, and quandaries in this assembly—after all, it's made up of *people*—but never think that these predicaments are beyond fixing or cleaning up. God is not going to reinvent the Church or start something else. What He started, He is well able to complete; and He is ever dealing with His people, standing (as John saw on Patmos) in the midst of the candlesticks[2] to build and perfect. The challenge of leading and supervising those of His Body is never too much for the Lord.

CHECK POINT: CHURCH LOVE

1. The Church is called the Church and bride of <u>Christ</u>.
   - *Romans 16:16; Revelation 19:7-9; 21:2, 9*

2. Believers become part of the Body of <u>Christ</u>.
   - *1 Corinthians 12:27; Ephesians 1:22-23*

3. <u>Christ</u> sanctified and cleansed the Church so He could present it to <u>Himself</u>.
   - *Ephesians 5:25-27*

4. In the communion, the cup is called the blood of <u>Christ</u> and the bread is called the body of <u>Christ</u>.
   - *1 Corinthians 10:16*

5. The Church is subject unto <u>Christ</u>.
   - *Ephesians 5:24*

6. God gave <u>Jesus</u> to be the Head over all things to the Church.
   - *Ephesians 1:22b*

Jesus Is the Focus

You have been baptized into a living Being who wants to be involved in everything concerning His Church. He holds and exercises the right to make all the decisions—He is God! Though He started the Church 2000 years ago, Jesus continues, through the Spirit, to operate in and over all of its innumerous activities.

I grew up as a PK (a pastor's kid) and I can tell you that regularly there arise circumstances in a church which cannot be fixed with an easy solution or a routine answer. Because we are dealing with people, problems develop that are sticky, awkward, multi-layered, and stump even the wisest among us. Yet I have witnessed that in those times, the best thing to do—actually, the only thing to do—is to call in the expert, Jesus. No, I am not talking about bowing your head and saying a methodical prayer. I am talking about literally getting in touch with the Master and hearing His voice on the matter. That kind of praying is different.

Over and over again, I have been amazed at the wisdom that comes from Jesus. Many times His answers are so simple and so obvious; we are just blind. Many times He tells us to do what we have been avoiding, and yet His directions always produce the optimum results. Yes, I can tell you that Jesus can and does handle the Church.

All too often, local assemblies go through unnecessary chaos and strain because in their dilemmas *the people fail to await Christ's answers*. In fact, it is in the hour of conflict when churches will veer off into false doctrine because they try handling things according to psychology, humanism, political vote, or even so-called common sense.

More churches need to awake to the fact that Jesus is running things, not them.

But it is not just the "big things" for which we need to seek intervention. Jesus is the foundation as well as the crowning peak of the Church. He is the starting line, but He is also the goal; and it is His inspiration that gives momentum and force to every-day life. Those who are His followers must learn to draw upon the Lord more and more and more. If there is one characteristic of a mature believer, it is that they are totally dependant on Jesus so that He gets constant glory!

Jesus has incredible multi-tasking power, and you as part of the Church, are to bring all of your needs to Him. Never seek another Heavenly figure for guidance or aid. Jesus is the supply in all aspects of your Christian walk. Your petitions will never overwhelm Him and He will never leave or abandon you. The Son of God can handle the pressure of being all-in-all.

CHECK POINT: ONE STOP

1.   Messiah feeds His flock.
     * *Isaiah 40:11*

2.   Jesus said that His sheep hear His voice and follow Him.
     * *Isaiah 49:8*

     Jesus is …

3.   … the Apostle and High Priest of our profession.
     * *Hebrews 3:1*

4.   … the Author and Finisher of Our Faith.
     * *Hebrews 12:2*

84

5. ... the Chief Cornerstone.
    - *1 Peter 2:6*
6. ... the Commander.
    - *Isaiah 55:4*
7. ... the Head of the Church.
    - *Ephesians 5:23*
8. ... the King of saints.
    - *Revelation 15:3*
9. ... the Shepherd and Bishop of our souls.
    - *1 Peter 2:25*

Kingdom Co-workers

The Church does not belong to man and essentially does not multiply by man; however, Christ utilizes man (yes, Christian minister, you are being used!).

Overlooking no aspect of His Church, Jesus hand picks people to work for Him, giving them divine abilities and platforms of responsibility for their individual assignment. This is what is known as an anointing. This anointing comes upon men and women alike, and is backed up by the authority of the Lord Himself.

There are many things to say about the anointing, but let me address that which pertains to Church leadership. Jesus is the one who raises up apostles, prophets, evangelists, pastors, and teachers for the Church. Should you receive an anointing for Church leadership, there are a couple things to keep in mind. First, there is no such thing as a ministry which is unique to you; and second, your Kingdom authority has nothing to do with your personal potential or even your enthusiasm. Whatever spiritual gifts and blessings you have, they are borrowed portions of the perfect anointing that was and is on the Lord Jesus Christ. He was and is everything to the Church; and what is more, He is the best, the Master of all ministries.

Let me explain it this way: if you have an anointing as an apostle, you are simply following Jesus in His mission.

- "He that receiveth you receiveth me, and he that receiveth me receiveth him that sent me." – Matthew 10:40

If you have authority as a prophet, you are moving in a realm which speaks of Jesus.

- "… for the testimony of Jesus is the spirit of prophecy." – Revelation 19:10b

If you have an anointing as an evangelist, you are exercising what evangelistic work Jesus is doing.

- "Behold, I stand at the door, and knock." – Revelation 3:20a

If you have an anointing as a pastor, you are operating in an office directly influenced by the vision of Jesus.

- "I am the good shepherd." – John 10:14

If you have an anointing as a teacher, you are showing others what Jesus is saying.

- "I have many things to say and to judge of you." – John 8:26a

The Lord takes His anointing very seriously; and it is for the sake of His anointing that He expects Church leadership to be received in His name. You are to honor them and to obey them as they speak His Word. Jesus made it very plain that if you do not accept those whom He sends, it is counted as you rejecting Him.

CHECK POINT: ENVOY

1. Jesus sets up leadership in the Church.
   - *Ephesians 4:10-11*

2. As the Father sent Jesus, Jesus sends us.
   - *John 20:21; Matthew 10:16*

3. We are workers together with Jesus.
   - *2 Corinthians 6:1*

4. Jesus works with those who preach the Gospel.
   - *Mark 16:20*

Jesus Settled Church Doctrine

What the Church should believe and practice was established by the Lord while He was here on earth; and this founding of ultimate truth was planned long before Jesus began to teach and preach in Israel.

As far back as Moses, God was setting the stage for His Son; for Moses admitted that his covenant would be disobeyed and turned away from,[3] but he prophesied,

> "The LORD thy God will raise up unto thee a Prophet from the midst of thee, of thy brethren, like unto me; <u>unto him ye shall hearken</u> ... [I] will put my words in his mouth; and he shall speak unto them all that I shall command him. And it shall come to pass, *that* whosoever will not hearken unto <u>my words which he shall speak in my name</u>, I will require *it* of him" – Deuteronomy 18:15, 18-19

The prophets saw Messiah Jesus as the Lawgiver also, for they declared,

> "... he will teach us of <u>his ways</u>, and we will walk in <u>his paths</u>: <u>for the law</u> shall go forth of Zion, <u>and the word of the LORD</u> from Jerusalem." – Micah 4:1-2

> "Behold my servant ... <u>he shall bring forth judgment to the Gentiles</u> ... <u>he shall bring forth judgment unto truth</u>. He shall not fail nor be discouraged, till he have set judgment in the earth: and <u>the isles shall wait for his law</u>." – Isaiah 42:1-4

Jesus' words are not merely nice ideals, reserved as optional exercises for the extra devoted who want to gain special spiritual credits. Jesus came to the entire world bringing the ultimate law of life. The Man of Galilee speaks the words of the Kingdom, words that are pregnant with power and promise; words which, when received in an obedient and trusting heart, bring forth the kind of fruit that

God desires in you: godliness, righteousness, honor, truth, and humility. This is why we Christians labor both to announce God's graciousness AND to convert people to the "law" that Jesus set forth.

When we accept the words of Jesus, we accept the glorious will of God, for the Heavenly Voice which was heard of the Apostles said,

"This is my beloved Son. <u>Hear ye Him</u>."
– Matthew 17:5

When we receive the Father's commandments through the Son, we receive the very life, the very divine nature[4] in which the Son walks. We get *His* strength, *His* faith, *His* love, *His* joy, *His* power, *His* holiness, and *His* faithfulness—imagine, *all of these are in His words.*

Jesus' words will never be matched in power or in authority. As a believer, realize that you have no obligation whatsoever to follow traditions or commandments laid down since the ministry of Christ. All you have to worry about is what you find in the pages of the Bible. Remember, you have not been baptized into man but into Jesus.

CHECK POINT: TRUE FAITH

1. God has spoken unto us in these last days <u>by *His*</u> Son.
   - *Hebrews 1:1-2*

2. <u>Jesus' words</u> are spirit and life.
   - *John 6:63*

3. Church beliefs are called the doctrines of <u>Christ</u>.
   - *Hebrews 6:1; 2 John 1:9*

4. Jesus taught that if someone keeps His "words" it proves they love Him; if someone does not keep His "sayings" it proves they do not love Him.

    *   *John 14:23-24; Luke 6:46; Matthew 7:21-23*

5. There is no other foundation than Jesus Christ.

    *   *1 Corinthians 3:11*

6. We are to let the word of Christ dwell in us.

    *   *Colossians 3:16*

7. We are to instruct everyone everywhere to observe Jesus' commandments.

    *   *Matthew 28:20*

8. At the end of the world, we will be judged by the words of Jesus.

    *   *John 12:48*

APPLICATION

A. The Church is your salvation: true or false?

B. Who is running the Church on earth?

C. Church leaders have the responsibility to define what the Church should or should not believe: true or false?

D. Are there Church leaders who fail or fall?

E. How should you respond when a leader fails or falls?

F. Please explain how baptism into Jesus is baptism into the Church.

G. What is the name you take on at baptism which identifies the Church?

H. What is your relationship to others in the Church?

Answers on page 142

Advanced Reading: "Appendix 6: Baptism and Church Unity" page 133

CHAPTER 8

JESUS IS THE HEIR TO THE KINGDOM

" Thou art my Son; this day have I begotten thee. – Psalms 2:7

On the Throne

God delegated the earth to mankind to rule over it;[1] but while we are attempting to master survival *from* the elements and comfort *with* the elements, we remain powerless *over* the elements. The reality is that in relation to the earth's operations, we are vastly insignificant. The same is true for the invisible, spiritual realm; we human beings are vulnerable and unimpressive. What rulership we can exercise on this planet turns out to be very, very limited.

On the other hand, Jesus (having received all rights and authority from the Father) exerts ideal dominion over everything. The wind, the sky, the waters, and the stars of the Heavens are all under Christ's strict supervision. The yield of the harvest, the offspring of bird and beast, the bounty of the sea, all of these are the inheritance of the Son of Man.

God has even given Him rule over all the affairs of mankind, not just those of Church people. Yes, Christians are His, but so are the unsaved. Governments, government leaders, nations, and continents are subject to Him; and kingdoms rise and fall in direct proportion to their relationship with Christ—whether or not they are aware of it. Whenever nations have submitted to His power and principles, there has been stability; and whenever those nations have exalted themselves apart from His paths, there has been decadence and even destruction. Ruling without democratic nomination, military might, or earthly politics, Jesus is the permanent sovereign of the world.

As people who are converted to the Son of God, our heritage, our roots, and our loyalty are now concentrated in the Kingdom. We have been adopted and adapted for a divine, earthly empire. As citizens of a Heavenly city and subjects of a Heavenly King, we are partakers of a growing world power, and our leader's name is Jesus.

CHECK POINT: INHERITANCE

1. The Kingdom of God is attributed to Jesus as being <u>His Kingdom</u>.
     - *2 Timothy 4:1; Ephesians 5:5; 2 Peter 1:11*

2. <u>Jesus</u> is the Heir of all Things
     - *Hebrews 1:2*

3. God exalted <u>Jesus</u> to divine power.
     - *Acts 5:31; Ephesians 1:20*

4. The Father has placed <u>Jesus</u> above <u>all</u> principalities, powers, mights, dominions, and names.
     - *Ephesians 1:21*

5. The kingdoms of this world are become *the kingdoms* of our Lord, <u>and of His Christ</u>; and <u>He shall reign</u> for ever.
     - *Revelation 11:15*

Jesus Has Priority

Suppose that you are at a playground with your little one and suppose that there are dozens of other children playing there, too. All of a sudden, you are aware that there is eminent danger and you must leave immediately. What do you do? Out of all the boys and girls there, you run towards your own child and scream out their name. Only when you have hold of your little one, do you turn your attention to the other kids.

Nothing but your individual sense of duty trained you to do that. It is not that you dislike other people's children; it is simply that your child is your main concern. Your child is your priority.

In the Kingdom of God, the Father gives Jesus rank above anyone and anything else. You have to understand this lest you get poisoned by the man-centered gospel that is currently polluting our churches. Yes, God loves you and cares for you, but the reputation of Christ's Kingdom and of the name of Jesus takes precedence over individual interests or pursuits. What this essentially means is, you cannot simply slap the label of your own sonship over personal sin, carnality, and downright selfishness and—voila!—it has God's clearance. Remember, Jesus is zealous about building a Church, to fill the earth with the glory of truth, with righteousness, and with a holy people. Anything that may contaminate or dilute the Son's project is censured and convicted by the Father. Christ has first priority.

As I was writing this chapter, I heard this prophecy in my spirit,

*"Who is going to hear my call?" says the Lord.
"Who is going to let me use them instead of the
other way around. For too long, you've tried to use
me. You've tried to fit me into your agenda, but I'll
not be used," says the Lord. "If anyone is going to
use anyone, I'm going to use you and do with you
as I please, for I am the Lord. I am your God. I am
your Master, not the other way around."*

Nothing in the Kingdom is about doing as you please or
how you wish to be placed in Christ's body. Jesus the King
puts His people where He wants them and then He tells
them what to do. So when the Lord calls you to something—
even something that goes against your personal wants—that
calling must take preeminence in your life *because it comes
by the One who has preeminence.*

In Jesus, your will is consumed and you are thrust into
His service—a magnificent honor! All you have to worry
about is doing your part. The risks, the provision, the
sacrifices, the losses, and all the pressure that is involved in
the performance of your calling are ultimately not yours.
They belong to the boss, Jesus; and when you do what He
has commanded, that is when the blessings come, for God
supports anything that belongs to the Heir! All of your
prayers and needs become urgent business in Heaven when
you are working in Christ's service.

CHECK POINT: FAVORITE

1. God's eternal purpose is in Jesus Christ.
    *   *Ephesians 3:11*

2. All people and all nations are to serve <u>Jesus</u>.
   - *Daniel 7:13-14*

3. You are a slave[2] of <u>Jesus Christ</u>.
   - *Colossians 3:24; Romans 14:17-18*

4. You are to labor that you may be accepted <u>of Jesus Christ</u>.
   - *2 Corinthians 5:9-10*

5. You must "crucify" your desires to belong to <u>Christ</u>.
   - *Galatians 5:24*

Jesus Is the One to be Reckoned With

Temporal or earthly blessings are not the only thing you will gain from obeying the reigning Jesus. There is coming a day when earth's prearranged existence will be timed out and life as we know will come to an end. That is when the conversion to and sacrifices for Christ will mean the most.

Jesus is coming again; and when He does, He will be looking for those who recognized His total authority and who allowed themselves to be monopolized by His perfect will. To them He will give the greatest of rewards, eternal life.

However, there is something else to think about. Those failing to comply with Christ's rights will be condemned to an eternal damnation without God. Jesus—the sympathetic Ruler who came for them, bled for them, suffered for them, and prayed for them—will be the One to sentence them. Never will there ever be a more fair trial.

As God who came to earth, Jesus' life had the most meaning and impact on this planet than anyone in history.

He is the One who started it all and He is the One who will be there at the end. To be in Him, in every sense of the phrase, is to be in life and for life to be in you.

Your one chance at immortality is to make peace with Jesus, for He is the one who will raise people from the dead to life everlasting. Your promise of resurrection is just one more reason you are baptized into the Lord Jesus Christ.

CHECK POINT: FINAL PHASE

1. Earth's climactic and final moment is referred to as <u>the Day and the Revelation of the Lord Jesus Christ</u>.
   - *1 Corinthians 1:8; 1 Peter 1:13*

2. On this day, <u>Jesus</u> will return in the clouds, and both the just and the unjust shall rise from the dead.
   - *Matthew 24:30; Acts 1:11; 24:15; Daniel 12:2*

3. <u>Jesus</u> will judge everyone, both the living and the dead. This is known as "the judgment seat of <u>Christ</u>."
   - *2 Timothy 4:1; 2 Corinthians 5:10*

4. The Father has committed all judgment to <u>the Son</u>.
   - *John 5:22*

5. <u>Jesus</u> shall reward every man according to their deeds.
   - *Matthew 16:24*

6. Even secrets, hidden things, and counsels of the heart will be judged <u>by Jesus</u>.
   - *Romans 2:16; 1 Corinthians 4:5*

7. <u>Jesus</u> shall take vengeance on the wicked by sending them to everlasting punishment by fire.
   - *2 Thessalonians 1:7-9; Matthew 25:41, 46*

8. <u>Jesus</u> shall be glorified in His saints and give them immortality.

   - *2 Thessalonians 1:10; John 3:15-16; 10:27-28*

APPLICATION

A. Is God's Kingdom opposite science? Explain.

B. Jesus is only interested in spiritual things and that is the scope of His inheritance: true or false?

C. Are institutions such as government, business, military, technology, entertainment, or education within the realm of Christ's authority?

D. Is Christ in any way obligated to man?

E. Give one word which is used to describe the length of time for both final punishment and final reward?

F. The devil sends people to Hell: true or false?

G. Since He is Savior of the world, Jesus hates judgment: true or false?

H. Do you as a believer have to be afraid of the end of the world?

Answers on page 142

Advanced Reading: "Appendix 7: The Question of Rebaptism" page 135

THE GLORY THAT IS FILLING THE EARTH

Solomon had a great insight, "Better is the end of a thing than the beginning thereof."[1] Concerning the Church, this indicates a happy ending to the Gospel's influence rather than a gloomy and depleted one. Final events will outshine the beginning ones. That being the case, the Book of Acts is not a standard to be reached but a history to be surpassed.

I believe that the present struggles and threats of the modern Body of Christ are not only familiar problems but problems bound to be overcome. While many complain that people are ignorant of or antagonistic against Christianity (and supposedly harder to reach), I say that this is not the hour to modify or water things down! God is setting the stage for a global awakening and this is the time to be as radical with the pure Gospel as ever before!

Even as I write this, there are news articles surfacing from Europe of churches that are seeing sudden growth and interest in Christianity. I am hearing reports from pastors and youth pastors across America of an up and coming generation who are showing surprising signs of devotion and integrity. All of us are reading about thousands of people the world over who are turning to Jesus Christ and praying for their nations.

The message of Jesus is what triggered world-wide awakening in the Early Church, it is what has spawned multitudes of revivals through the ages, and *it is what will shake the earth again.* For this reason I have written to you, because Jesus is coming to His house, looking for those with faith in Him, and conquering all His enemies. No, I am not referring to Christ's Second Coming; I am speaking of something before that, something that so many of us feel and see in the Spirit for the very near future. The world as we know it is about to be changed, turned upside down by a return to the original Gospel.

Now is the time to be prepared, not with a life enhancement message and not with a neat little program for increasing church membership. Impersonal religious fads fade as quickly as they come. No, now is the time to be prepared with *Jesus,* His "now" power and His "now" Kingdom. He is the momentum of the Church which cannot be stopped; and every time He is lifted up, He draws a hungry world to His bridegroom table.

In these last days, the best is yet to come. We are about to see a greater demonstration of the Holy Ghost and a greater influx of converts than ever before. Why? Because there is a greater chorus throughout the world calling on the name that pulls down all strongholds, the name that defines the Church, the name that has been exalted above all others:

JESUS!

APPENDICES

INFANT CONVERSION?

I want to make this as simple as it is, because infant baptism is more often than not a subject complicated by speculation, tradition, and opinion.

First

The New Testament *does* show that the faith of the parents sanctifies the children (1 Corinthians 7:14).

I grew up in a Christian home, and I experienced two essentials that hallow or purify something: the Word of God and prayer.[1] Along with my siblings, I heard the Scriptures quoted on a regular basis, and I learned from Dad and Mom's lifestyle what walking out the Bible looked like. Because of a domestic atmosphere of prayer, I remember feeling the presence of God at a very young age and I witnessed miracles, answers to prayer, and divine intervention—right in our home. In fact, the biggest influence to my own consecration was a direct result of the godliness lived out by my parents.

I can assure you that it was their faith, not mine, which brought the spiritual and natural blessings I enjoyed throughout my childhood.

Second

Make no mistake, in every heart there must be eventual, personal belief[2] in the Lord Jesus Christ.

For me, there came a point where I had to choose God's salvation personally. While there were several spiritual experiences I had as a boy, one of the first was at the age of 11. I was watching an evangelist on television at a friend's house. The evangelist began to talk about rededicating your life to Christ, and I knew at that pre-teen time that I was a sinner and that I needed to repent of certain things. I prayed along with the evangelist and left my friend's home changed. I began loving my brothers and sister, obeying my parents, and I also began reading my Bible and praying. Later that year, knowing full well what I was doing, I was baptized.

Dads and Moms, let me tell you something. As much as you may love your children, you cannot be a Christian for them. You can be a spiritual covering for them, you can pray for them, you can bless them, and you can train them; but you will never have the legitimate power to believe for them, repent for them, or make confession of sins for them. *No one* in the Bible *ever* used or talked about water baptism as a means of blessing someone or as a preventative imposed upon another to guarantee their future conversion. Somewhere along their time line, your children have to embrace Jesus Christ and be baptized into Him *all by themselves.*

The Old Covenant circumcision (being in the skin or the flesh) required no belief, no permission from the male candidate. However, the New Covenant, being so much better, is based on faith and therefore has a circumcision—water baptism into Jesus[3]—which requires deliberate belief in the heart. This is how Christian women can be considered circumcised but it is also why believers who are voluntarily baptized are more likely to be strong in their faith.

To tell a person that they are a Christian just because he or she underwent infant baptism is to give that individual false hope and to prevent them from exercising necessary faith to be saved. Faith, not a ceremony, appeases God.

One final thing: growing up in church, I have witnessed many people dedicate their little ones to the Lord, as did Hanna. This, however, is quite different from baptizing an infant. First, child dedication is a plea for the Lord to watch over our offspring; second (and most important), this is a promise to God that the parents will raise their boy or girl in the way of righteousness and faith.

While your children cannot be converted by you, they can certainly be covered by you.

DOES BAPTISM SAVE?

Mark 16:16 is one of those passages that has become unnecessarily controversial, and basically it is because people are ignorant of its cultural and customary background. I am talking of the verse where Jesus said,

> "He that believeth and is baptized shall be saved; but he that believeth not shall be damned."

Some people quote this verse to claim that one cannot go to Heaven without being immersed in water. To them, it does not matter that one has repented and called on the name of the Lord for forgiveness; unless a person has undergone baptism, they are not saved. Those who hold this view go so far as to say that the thief on the cross who defended the Lord remained unsaved because he never underwent baptism—even though the one called SALVATION said, "To day shalt thou be with me in paradise." [1]

In all honesty, you can see how people would come to this defective conclusion. The language of this verse does seem to make baptism a qualification of eternal life. However, this conclusion is really backwards as well as oversimplified. To discern the significance of Christ's saying here, you have to be aware of the context of both the Scriptures and the custom itself.

There are three things that can bring the bubble back to the middle for us.

1. Jesus did not come to institute a system of religious, formal procedures. He abhorred ceremonial and traditional practice as being the means for one's justification. And concerning water immersion, Jesus was promoting something much greater than the ritual itself as a qualification for salvation.

2. It is not that there is no system or policy, it is just that *Jesus* is the system and the policy; this is another detail people overlook in this verse. Jesus Himself is SALVATION and *it is in His name that repentance and remission of sins are to be preached.*[2] Anybody can go underwater for repentance or use water try to cleanse their soul (as the heathen still do today). Biblical baptism, though, is connected with confessing sins,[3] washing away sins, remission of sins, and calling upon the Lord,[4] *because it is connected to Jesus.* Jesus is what and who saves! He is the power of water baptism! His blood, His death, and His resurrection are the keys that have unlocked faith and have separated Christian baptism from becoming an empty rite of passage.

Actually, the water with the blood and the Spirit, all speak of Jesus; and all three of these steps—corporately and individually—are meant to be your marriage, your leap of faith, your conversion to Him. The opposite is true as well:

to deliberately avoid the water as well as the blood and the Spirit, is to shun not symbolic practice, but Jesus Himself.

3. The greatest oversight here, however, is the biblical practice of water baptism as being discipleship to Jesus. Only when one recognizes this correlation can the weight of both baptism and the above verse be grasped.

Allow me to amplify Mark 16:16 with the biblical understanding of baptism in mind—that it is coupled with discipleship—and show you how baptism and being saved tie in. This is how the early disciples would have understood Jesus' words.

> "He that believeth and is baptized [*becomes my disciple, converts to me, is totally sold out to who I am and what I am bringing*] shall be saved; but he that believeth not [*to the extent that they refuse to be immersed in me, refuse to follow my commandments and principles, and refuse to be my disciple*] shall be damned."

Mark 16:16 clearly fits in with the New Testament principle that "faith without works is dead." Faith and conversion go together. You cannot choose to have Jesus take away your sins and yet walk away from His universal call to be His disciple. It just does not work that way. You cannot say, "I like the cross part; but I'll pass on the servant/follower thing." Jesus is an all-or-nothing Savior!

To say that the ritual of baptism saves is wrong. On the other hand, to say that a rejection of discipleship (via baptism) will bring *not* damnation is absolutely wrong as well. It seems to be a fine line at first, but again, the big difference is that the Kingdom is decisively about a "Him" and never an "it."

JESUS' NAME IS ALWAYS VALID

For the first 100 plus years of New Testament ministry, all Christian saints were baptized in the name of Jesus with the understanding that they were identifying themselves with Christ.

However, beginning in the Second Century, changes began to take place. Slowly, men influenced by Greek philosophy took it upon themselves to dissect and rationalize the otherwise simple faith of Jesus Christ. They developed their own ideas of Christ, of God, and of baptism; and by the Fourth Century, Church leaders were ready to impose these ideas on all who called themselves Christians.

In 381 A.D., 150 bishops assembled in Constantinople; and, assuming an authority over the entire believing world, the "fathers" drew up a document that, among other things, officially condemned those who baptized in the name of Jesus.[1]

What the first believers in Jesus joyfully accepted—and, I might add, that to which the Holy Ghost had bore witness—Church leaders blacklisted as being not merely unpopular but wrong, erroneous, and cursed![2] From that council to this very day, Church leaders have excommunicated and condemned those who followed the original pattern of water baptism.

The Bottom Line

Truth is unchangeable, and what was true in Bible days is still true today. The same goes for sin. What the Bible condemned yesterday, it still condemns today. So, does God through His Word condemn or condone water baptism in Jesus' name? If God rejects it, then the matter is settled; and a man who practices such is a rebel and a fraud. Yet if God does not condemn this baptism, then a man is free from any curse by any man.

Since they all baptized in Jesus' name, were the Apostles heretics? If they were, then the book of Acts is an exposé of corrupted ministers who promoted false doctrine! If Peter, Paul, Philip, and the rest were heretics then the whole New Testament Church had a foundation of error, nonconformity, and sin.

If baptism in Jesus' name is heresy, then this practice of the Apostles automatically disqualifies the authority of their writings. We should cut out from our Bibles all of Paul's epistles (because Paul baptized in Jesus' name), 1 and 2 Peter (because Peter baptized in Jesus' name), and Mark (because he was a disciple of Peter). In fact, we should ban all the New Testament writings because *all their authors baptized in Jesus' name!*

Everyone who has read the New Testament knows that the Apostles were never rebuked by any Church leader for baptizing in Jesus' name nor did they ever grieve the Holy Ghost, for God bore witness with great power that what the Apostles were preaching and doing were His very will. My

Bible says that God was working with the Apostles "confirming the word with signs following."[3]

A man with any kind of common sense knows that if he is going to build something—a house, a business, or even a position of authority—he must build it right *from the beginning*. It would be foolish for him to begin something that he would eventually have to tear down and redo. God is no fool. He did not begin baptism in Jesus' name and later on decide to call it heresy. Praise the Lord, the Church is not built on heretics or heresy!

The fact that God did not readjust this practice should by itself show you and me that baptism in Jesus' name is actually *original divine intent*. If the Apostles practiced baptism in Jesus' name, so can we and so must we. The reverse is true, too: if the Apostles did not condemn this kind of baptism, neither should we. The Bible says, we are "built upon the foundation of the apostles and prophets, Jesus Christ himself being the chief corner *stone*."[4] We are not built on the votes of Church councils, the exclamations of ecclesiastical creeds, or even on the so-called "church fathers." Our bedrock is on the teachings of Christ and on the Apostles who preached those teachings. Hallelujah!

Conclusion

What really happened in Constantinople is that a group of Church leaders got together with the apparent notion that they had become important enough to redo, or rather, outdo what God had established. However honorable their intentions might have been or whatever difficulties they may have been facing, nothing justifies their attempt to reinvent

Biblical revelation and supplant Biblical practice. Men, not God, have said that baptizing in Jesus' name was a heresy!

> "How shall I curse, whom God hath not cursed? or how shall I defy, *whom* the LORD hath not defied?" – Numbers 23:8

Yet, even though the Constantinople decision continues to blind the eyes and minds of religious leaders to the great revelation and power of baptism in Jesus' name, the standing biblical principle is that the end of something is better than its beginning.[5] God is not going to allow His final work to degenerate and mutate from what it was, but before the end He is going to cause it to dominate. Truth will come around full circle; and by the Word of the Lord I can tell you that prior to Jesus returning, the world will see the true Church put away all its non-biblical traditions to obtain the original and best which is in Jesus Christ.

THE LIST

A few years ago, I put together a booklet which, in my mind, incredibly strengthens (if not solves) the case for water baptism in Jesus' name. Originally entitled *301 Shouts for Being Baptized in Jesus' Name*, it revealed the particular prominence that has been placed upon the Lord Jesus Christ by the Holy Spirit, who inspired both the Old and New Testament writers. That list is the basis for this book, though here it has been modified, condensed, and dispersed.

In order to emphasize the biblical revelation that all the blessings are in Jesus and that the Father has delivered all things into His hands, I am producing for you that original *301 Shouts* list. Go over it, pray for revelation, and grow in the knowledge of Jesus Christ.

WE ARE COMMANDED TO ...

1. Give thanks for all things in Jesus' name.
   * *Ephesians 5:20*
2. Continually offer the sacrifices of praise to God by Christ Jesus.
   * *Hebrews 13:15*
3. Reckon ourselves alive unto God through Jesus Christ.
   * *Romans 6:11*
4. Let the word of Christ dwell in us.
   * *Colossians 3:16*

5. To be found of Christ in peace, without spot, and blameless.
   - *2 Peter 3:14*
6. Grow up into Christ in all things.
   - *Ephesians 4:15*
7. Grow in the knowledge of Jesus Christ.
   - *2 Peter 3:18*
8. Walk in Christ Jesus.
   - *Colossians 2:6*
9. To abide in Christ Jesus.
   - *1 John 2:28*

THE BIBLE SAYS ...

10. We are heirs of God, and joint-heirs with Christ.
    - *Romans 8:17a*
11. The saints are to be glorified with Jesus.
    - *Romans 8:17b*
12. Jesus Christ is in us.
    - *2 Corinthians 13:5*
13. The Law was our schoolmaster to bring us to Christ.
    - *Galatians 3:24*
14. The law was the covenant that was confirmed before of God in Christ.
    - *Galatians 3:17*
15. We are taught by Christ.
    - *Ephesians 4:20-21*
16. If we abide in the Son of God we will not sin.
    - *1 John 3:6*
17. Christ has made us free.
    - *Galatians 5:1*
18. The Church is subject unto Christ.
    - *Ephesians 5:24*
19. We are reconciled to God by the flesh of Jesus.
    - *Colossians 1:21-22*
20. Your life is hid with Christ in God.
    - *Colossians 3:3*
21. We shall appear with Jesus in glory.
    - *Colossians 3:4*
22. Paul prayed that the name of our Lord Jesus Christ would be glorified in the saints.
    - *2 Thessalonians 1:11-12*
23. We are called to obtain the glory of our Lord Jesus Christ.
    - *2 Thessalonians 2:14*
24. The blood of Jesus purges our conscience.
    - *Hebrews 9:14*

25. <u>Christ</u> entered into heaven to appear before God for us.
    - *Hebrews 9:24*
26. The kingdoms of this world are become *the kingdoms* of our Lord, <u>and of his Christ</u>; and <u>he shall reign</u> for ever.
    - *Revelation 11:15*
27. God was in <u>Christ</u>, reconciling the world unto himself.
    - *2 Corinthians 5:19*
28. If we know the love of <u>Christ</u> we will be filled with all the fullness of God.
    - *Ephesians 3:19*

WITH JESUS...

29. We are quickened from sins.
    - *Ephesians 2:5*
30. We shall live together.
    - *1 Thessalonians 5:10*
31. We shall reign.
    - *2 Timothy 2:12*

IN JESUS ...

32. We are chosen from the foundation of the world.
    - *Ephesians 1:4*
33. Is our redemption.
    - *Romans 3:24*
34. There is no condemnation.
    - *Romans 8:1*
35. We have boldness and access with confidence.
    - *Ephesians 3:12*
36. Is the law of the Spirit of Life.
    - *Romans 8:2*
37. Nothing can separate us from the love of God.
    - *Romans 8:39*
38. The love of God is perfected.
    - *1 John 2:5*
39. We are one body.
    - *Romans 12:5*
40. We are sanctified.
    - *1 Corinthians 1:2*
41. We are wise.
    - *1 Corinthians 4:10*
42. All shall be made alive.
    - *1 Corinthians 15:22*
43. God stablisheth us and anoints us.
    - *2 Corinthians 1:21*
44. We triumph.
    - *2 Corinthians 2:14*
45. The veil is done away.
    - *2 Corinthians 3:1*
46. We are a new creature.
    - *2 Corinthians 5:17*

47. Is the simplicity of the Gospel.
    - *2 Corinthians 11:3*
48. Is our liberty.
    - *Galatians 2:4*
49. We are children of God by faith in Christ Jesus
    - *Galatians 3:26*
50. All (Jews, Greeks, etc.) are one.
    - *Galatians 3:28*
51. Was and is the working of God's mighty power.
    - *Ephesians 1:19-20*
52. We are raised up and made to sit in heavenly places.
    - *Ephesians 2:6*
53. We are the workmanship of God, created unto good works.
    - *Ephesians 2:10*
54. We are made nigh to God by His blood.
    - *Ephesians 2:13*
55. The Gentiles are fellow heirs, partakers of the promise of the Gospel.
    - *Ephesians 3:6*
56. Is God's eternal purpose.
    - *Ephesians 3:11*
57. Is the prize of the high calling of God.
    - *Philippians 3:14*

58. We are complete.
    - *Colossians 2:10*
59. Is faith and love.
    - *1 Timothy 1:14*
60. Is the promise of life.
    - *2 Timothy 1:1*
61. We are given purpose.
    - *2 Timothy 1:9*
62. Is grace.
    - *2 Timothy 2:1*
63. Is salvation unto eternal glory.
    - *2 Timothy 2:10*
64. Is every good thing.
    - *Philemon 1:6*
65. Is our good conversation.
    - *1 Peter 3:16*
66. We are in him that is true.
    - *1 John 5:20*
67. We are preserved.
    - *Jude 1:1*

BY JESUS ...

68. Came grace and truth.
    - *John 1:17*
69. God shall judge the secrets of men.
    - *Romans 2:16*
70. Grace reigns through righteousness unto eternal life.
    - *Romans 5:21*
71. Our consolation aboundeth.

- *2 Corinthians 1:5*
72. We are predestinated unto the adoption of children.
  - *Ephesians 1:5*
73. Are the fruits of righteousness.
  - *Philippians 1:11*
74. We offer up spiritual sacrifices, acceptable to God.
  - *1 Peter 2:5*

THROUGH JESUS ...

75. Is the resurrection from the dead.
  - *Acts 4:2*
76. We have trust to God-ward.
  - *2 Corinthians 3:4*
77. The blessing of Abraham comes on the Gentiles.
  - *Galatians 3:14*
78. We are no more servants but sons, heirs of God.
  - *Galatians 4:7*
79. God showed the exceeding riches of his grace in kindness towards us.
  - *Ephesians 2:7*
80. God shall keep our hearts and minds.
  - *Philippians 4:7*

81. God abundantly shed the Holy Ghost on us.
  - *Titus 3:5-6*
82. God is working in us that which is wellpleasing in His sight.
  - *Hebrews 13:21*
83. We come to God.
  - *Hebrews 7:25*

JESUS CHRIST IS ...

84. The Advocate
  - *1 John 2:1*
85. The Almighty
  - *Revelation 1:8*
86. Alpha and Omega
  - *Revelation 1:8*
87. The Amen
  - *Revelation 3:14*
88. The Angel of His Presence
  - *Isaiah 63:9*
89. The Anointed
  - *Psalms 2:2*
90. The Apostle and High Priest of Our Profession
  - *Hebrews 3:1*
91. The Arm of the Lord
  - *Isaiah 51:9-10*
92. The Author and Finisher of Our Faith
  - *Hebrews 12:2*

93. The Beginning and End of the Creation of God
    - *Revelation 22:13*
94. The Beloved
    - *Ephesians 1:6*
95. The Branch
    - *Zechariah 3:8*
96. The Bread of Life
    - *John 6:48*
97. The Bridegroom
    - *Matthew 9:15*
98. The Bright and Morning Star
    - *Revelation 22:16*
99. The Brightness of the Father's Glory
    - *Hebrews 1:3*
100. The Captain of the Lord's Host
    - *Joshua 5:14*
101. The Captain of Salvation
    - *Hebrews 2:10*
102. The Chief Cornerstone
    - *1 Peter 2:6*
103. Chiefest Among Ten Thousand
    - *Song of Songs 5:10*
104. The Chosen of God
    - *1 Peter 2:4*
105. The Christ
    - *Matthew 16:20*
106. Christ of God
    - *Luke 9:20*
107. The Commander
    - *Isaiah 55:4*
108. The Consolation of Israel
    - *Luke 2:25*
109. The Counsellor
    - *Isaiah 9:6*
110. The Covenant of the People
    - *Isaiah 42:6*
111. David
    - *Jeremiah 30:9*
112. The Daysman
    - *Job 9:33*
113. The Dayspring
    - *Luke 1:78*
114. The Day Star
    - *2 Peter 1:19*
115. The Deliverer
    - *Romans 11:26*
116. The Desire of All Nations
    - *Haggai 2:7*
117. The Door
    - *John 10:7*
118. The Elect
    - *Isaiah 42:1*
119. Emmanuel, God with us
    - *Matthew 1:23*
120. The Ensign
    - *Isaiah 11:10*
121. Eternal life
    - *1 John 5:20*
122. Everlasting Father
    - *Isaiah 9:6*
123. The Faithful and True Witness

- *Revelation 3:14*
124. The First and Last
     - *Revelation 22:13*
125. The First Begotten of the Dead
     - *Revelation 1:5*
126. The Firstborn
     - *Psalms 89:27*
127. The Foundation
     - *Isaiah 28:16*
128. The Fountain
     - *Zechariah 13:1*
129. The Forerunner
     - *Hebrews 6:20*
130. The Gift of God
     - *John 4:10*
131. The Glory of Israel
     - *Luke 2:32*
132. God Blessed Forever
     - *Romans 9:5*
133. God Manifest in the Flesh
     - *1 Timothy 3:16*
134. The God of Israel
     - *Isaiah 45:15*
135. The God of the Whole Earth
     - *Isaiah 54:5*
136. God our Savior
     - *1 Timothy 2:3*
137. God's Dear Son
     - *Colossians 1:13*
138. The Good Master
     - *Matthew 19:16*
139. The Governor
     - *Matthew 2:6*
140. Head of the Church

- *Ephesians 5:23*
141. The Heir of all Things
     - *Hebrews 1:2*
142. The Head of Every Man
     - *1 Corinthians 11:3*
143. The Head of the Corner
     - *Matthew 21:42*
144. The Holy Child
     - *Acts 4:30*
145. The Holy One of God
     - *Mark 1:24*
146. The Holy One of Israel
     - *Isaiah 41:14*
147. Our Hope
     - *1 Timothy 1:1*
148. The Horn of Salvation
     - *Luke 1:69*
149. The I Am
     - *John 8:58*
150. The Image of God
     - *Hebrews 1:3*
151. Israel
     - *Isaiah 49:3*
152. Jehovah
     - *Isaiah 40:3*
153. Jehovah's Fellow
     - *Zechariah 13:7*
154. The Just One
     - *Acts 22:14*
155. The Just Person
     - *Matthew 27:24*
156. King of Israel
     - *John 1:49*
157. King of the Jews
     - *Matthew 2:2*
158. King of Saints

- *Revelation 15:3*
159. King of Kings
     - *1 Timothy 6:15*
160. King of Glory
     - *Psalms 24:10*
161. King of Zion
     - *Matthew 21:5*
162. King over All The Earth
     - *Zechariah 14:9*
163. The Lamb of God
     - *John 1:29*
164. The Lawgiver
     - *Isaiah 33:22*
165. The Leader
     - *Isaiah 55:4*
166. Life
     - *John 14:6*
167. The Everlasting Light
     - *Isaiah 60:20*
168. The Light of the World
     - *John 8:12*
169. The Light to the Gentiles
     - *Isaiah 42:6*
170. The True Light
     - *John 1:9*
171. The Living Bread
     - *John 6:51*
172. The Living Stone
     - *1 Peter 2:4*
173. The Lion of the Tribe of Judah
     - *Revelation 5:5*
174. Lord of Lords
     - *Revelation 19:16*
175. Lord of All

- *Acts 10:36*
176. The Lord our Righteousness
     - *Jeremiah 23:6*
177. The Lord God Almighty
     - *Revelation 15:3*
178. The Lord from Heaven
     - *1 Corinthians 15:47*
179. The Lord of Glory
     - *James 2:1*
180. The Lord of Hosts
     - *Isaiah 44:6*
181. The Lord, Mighty in Battle
     - *Psalms 24:8*
182. Lord of the Dead and Living
     - *Romans 14:9*
183. Lord of the Sabbath
     - *Mark 2:28*
184. Lord Over All
     - *Romans 10:12*
185. The Lord's Christ
     - *Luke 2:26*
186. The Lord Strong and Mighty
     - *Psalms 24:8*
187. The Lord, Your Holy One
     - *Isaiah 43:15*
188. The Lord, Your Redeemer
     - *Isaiah 43:14*
189. The Man Christ Jesus
     - *1 Timothy 2:5*

190. The Man of Sorrows
   • *Isaiah 53:3*
191. The Master
   • *Matthew 23:8*
192. The Mediator
   • *1 Timothy 2:5*
193. The Messenger of the Covenant
   • *Malachi 3:1*
194. Messiah the Prince
   • *Daniel 9:25*
195. The Mighty God
   • *Isaiah 9:6*
196. The Mighty one of Israel
   • *Isaiah 30:29*
197. The Mighty one of Jacob
   • *Isaiah 49:26*
198. Mighty to Save
   • *Isaiah 63:1*
199. The Minister of the Sanctuary
   • *Hebrews 8:2*
200. The Most Holy
   • *Daniel 9:24*
201. The Most Mighty
   • *Psalms 45:3*
202. The Nazarene
   • *Matthew 2:23*
203. The Only Begotten of the Father
   • *John 1:14*
204. The Only Wise God
   • *Jude 1:25*
205. The Passover
   • *1 Corinthians 5:7*

206. The Plant of Renown
   • *Ezekiel 34:29*
207. The Blessed and Only Potentate
   • *1 Timothy 6:15*
208. The Power of God
   • *1 Corinthians 1:24*
209. The Physician
   • *Matthew 9:12*
210. The Precious Cornerstone
   • *Isaiah 28:16*
211. The Prince of Life
   • *Acts 3:15*
212. The Prince of Peace
   • *Isaiah 9:6*
213. The Prince of the Kings of the Earth
   • *Revelation 1:5*
214. The Prophet
   • *Deuteronomy 18:15,18*
215. The Propitiation for Our Sins
   • *1 John 2:2*
216. Rabboni
   • *John 20:16*
217. The Ransom
   • *1 Timothy 2:6*
218. The Redeemer
   • *Isaiah 59:20*
219. The Resurrection and Life
   • *John 11:25*
220. Redemption
   • *1 Corinthians 1:30*
221. The Righteous Branch

- *Jeremiah 23:5*
222. The Righteous Judge
  - *2 Timothy 4:8*
223. The Righteous Servant
  - *Isaiah 53:11*
224. Righteousness
  - *1 Corinthians 1:30*
225. The Rock
  - *1 Corinthians 10:4*
226. The Root of David
  - *Revelation 5:5*
227. The Root of Jesse
  - *Isaiah 11:10*
228. The Rose of Sharon
  - *Song of Songs 2:1*
229. The Ruler in Israel
  - *Micah 5:2*
230. Salvation
  - *Luke 2:30*
231. Sanctification
  - *1 Corinthians 1:30*
232. The Sanctuary
  - *Isaiah 8:14*
233. Savior of the Body
  - *Ephesians 5:23*
234. Savior of the World
  - *1 John 4:14*
235. The Sceptre
  - *Numbers 24:17*
236. The Second Man Adam
  - *1 Corinthians 15:47*
237. The Seed of David
  - *2 Timothy 2:8*
238. The Seed of the Woman
  - *Genesis 3:15*
239. The Shepherd and Bishop of Our Souls
  - *1 Peter 2:25*
240. The Chief Shepherd
  - *1 Peter 5:4*
241. The Good Shepherd
  - *John 10:11*
242. The Great Shepherd
  - *Hebrews 13:20*
243. The Shepherd of Israel
  - *Psalms 80:1*
244. Shiloh
  - *Genesis 49:10*
245. The Son of the Father
  - *2 John 1:3*
246. The Son of God
  - *Multiple verses*
247. The Son of Man
  - *Multiple verses*
248. The Son of the Blessed
  - *Mark 14:61*
249. The Son of the Highest
  - *Luke 1:32*
250. The Son of David
  - *Matthew 9:27*
251. The Star
  - *Numbers 24:17*
252. The Sun of Righteousness
  - *Malachi 4:2*
253. The Surety of a Better Testament
  - *Hebrews 7:22*
254. The Stone

- *Matthew 21:42*
255. The Sure Foundation
- *Isaiah 28:16*
256. The Teacher
- *John 3:2*
257. The True God
- *1 John 5:20*
258. The Truth
- *John 14:6*
259. The Unspeakable Gift
- *2 Corinthians 9:15*
260. The Vine
- *John 15:1*
261. The Way
- *John 14:6*
262. He Which Is, Which Was, and Which Is To Come
- *Revelation 1:4*
263. The Wisdom of God
- *1 Corinthians 1:24*
264. Wonderful
- *Isaiah 9:6*
265. The Word of God
- *Revelation 19:13*
266. The Word of Life
- *1 John 1:1*

CONCERNING BAPTISM

267. The Bible reveals that we are baptized into Jesus Christ.
- *Romans 6:3*
268. Baptism is identified with Jesus' resurrection.

- *Romans 6:4*
269. As death was defeated, baptism into Jesus destroys the body of sin.
- *Romans 6:6; Galatians 2:20*
270. Baptism is called the Circumcision of Christ.
- *Colossians 2:11-12*

IN JESUS' NAME ...

271. Shall the Gentiles trust
- *Matthew 12:21*
272. Christ draw nears to gathering believers.
- *Matthew 18:20*
273. Saints work miracles.
- *Mark 16:17-18; Acts 3:6,16*
274. Repentance and remission of sins is preached.
- *Luke 24:47; Acts 2:38*
275. Your sins are forgiven.
- *1 John 2:12*
276. Forgiveness of sins was witnessed by the prophets.
- *Acts 10:43*
277. Believers have power to become the sons of God.

- *John 1:12*
278. God will answer prayer.
  - *John 14:14; John 16:26*
279. Believers have life.
  - *John 20:31*
280. We are washed (baptized!), sanctified, and justified.
  - *1 Corinthians 6:11*
281. The prophets have spoken.
  - *James 5:10*

AND ...

282. God hath highly exalted Jesus' name above every name.
  - *Philippians 2:9*

FURTHER MORE, THE BIBLE SAYS ...

283. Christ is all in all.
  - *Colossians 3:11*
284. The whole family in heaven and in earth is named by the name our Lord Jesus Christ.
  - *Ephesians 3:14-15*

285. All power is given to Jesus.
  - *Matthew 28:18; John 3:35*
286. All spiritual blessing in heavenly places are in Christ.
  - *Ephesians 1:3*
287. All things are of Jesus, through Jesus, and to Jesus.
  - *Romans 11:36*
288. All things in heaven and in earth are gathered together in Christ.
  - *Ephesians 1:10*
289. All our needs are supplied according to God's riches in glory by Christ Jesus.
  - *Philippians 4:19*
290. All the treasures of wisdom and knowledge are in Christ.
  - *Colossians 2:2-3*
291. In all things, God is to be glorified through Jesus.
  - *1 Peter 4:11*
292. All sin is cleansed by the blood of Jesus.
  - *1 John 1:7*
293. All things - that are in heaven, and that are in earth, visible and invisible, whether *they*

---

* Modern translations do away with Jesus' name here - a grave failure

be thrones, or dominions, or principalities, or powers - were created by him, and for him.
- *Colossians 1:16*

294. He is before all things.
- *Colossians 1:17*

295. All things consist by Him.
- *Colossians 1:17*

296. In all things, He has preeminence.
- *Colossians 1:18*

297. All things are to be done in the name of the Lord Jesus.
- *Colossians 3:17*

298. All the fulness of the Godhead dwelleth bodily in Him.
- *Colossians 2:9*

FINALLY ...

299. Jesus said, "Go ye therefore, and teach all nations, baptizing them in the **NAME** of the Father, and of the Son, and of the Holy Ghost." (*Matthew 28:19*) What is that name? The name of Jesus!
- In what name do we approach the Father? JESUS! *John 16:23-27*
- By what name do we know the Son? JESUS! *Matthew 1:22-23*
   Through what name do we receive the baptism of the Holy Ghost? JESUS! *John 14:26*

300. The Apostles obeyed Jesus' command, and in right revelation the entire Early Church Age baptized the new converts in Jesus' name. *Acts 2:38; 8:16; 9:4-5; 10:47-48; 19:5*

301. "Neither is there salvation in any other: for there is none other name under heaven given among men, whereby we MUST be saved."
- *Acts 4:12*

ACCUSATIONS AGAINST JESUS

The Gospels record that on one occasion James and John (the Sons of Zebedee and Jesus' disciples) approached the Lord and asked if the two of them they could sit each side of His throne. Jesus denied their request but asked them a curious question, "Are ye able to be baptized with the baptism I am baptized with?"[1] By His baptism He meant His crucifixion;[2] but by their baptism He meant Christian persecution itself. Jesus wanted to see if the two brothers would be willing to share with Him in giving their life for the Kingdom. He wanted to see how deep their dedication was to Him. James and John chose to be baptized with Christ.

No matter what you do in this life, you are always going to have enemies! Even as a Christian, you had better be prepared for this shocking reality. Do not expect your good, wholesome, godly intensions to be a magic key that will cause everyone to treat you nicely or fairly. No matter what excellent grace you have experienced from God and no matter what wonderful changes have taken place in your life, being a fervent disciple of Jesus of Nazareth is something which the world hardly counts as being agreeable. Why? Because, when the day is done, those who are in darkness do not love the commanding light of Jesus.

I would rather be up front about this truth of your baptism because I do not believe that in the end you would appreciate a sanitized version of the Gospel. On the contrary, I believe that in having a complete picture of the Christian life and in making an intelligent, deliberate decision for Christ Jesus, you, like James and John, will be all the better and stronger for it.

We all know the end and the victory of Jesus' earthly ministry, but what most of us may be unaware of is what kind of "baptism" the Lord had to endure—even before the cross. Take a look at the slanderous things Jesus' enemies accused Him of and keep in mind that none of these hindered Jesus from fulfilling His mission. You may recognize some of these as being accusations against you.

1. **Arrogant** *(insinuated)* Matthew 13:54-57

2. **Friend of or partner with sinners** Matthew 11:19

3. **Blasphemer** Matthew 9:3

4. **Criminal** John 18:30

5. **Deceiver** John 7:12

6. **Destroyer of the Temple** Matthew 26:61

7. **Exorcist by means of witchcraft** Matthew 12:24

8. **Failed Savior** Mark 15:31

9. **False Prophet** John 7:52

10. **Glutton** Matthew 11:19

11. **Imposter** John 9:28-29

12. **Insane** Mark 3:21

13. **Not of God** John 9:16

14. **Political Extremist and Activist** Luke 23:2

15. **Possessed with an unclean spirit, a devil** Mark 3:30; John 8:52

16. **Rabble-rouser** *(insinuated)* John 7:47-49

17. **Rebel** Luke 23:2

18. **Sabbath Breaker** (*and therefore a breaker of the Law of Moses*) Luke 6:2

19. **Samaritan** (*implying that He was a bastard as well as a corrupter*) John 8:48

20. **Self-promoter** John 8:13

21. **Sinner** John 9:24

22. **Tax evader** Luke 23:2

23. **Trouble maker** Luke 23:5

24. **Usurper** Mark 11:27-28

25. **Winebibber or alcoholic** Matthew 11:19

26. **Worthy of Death** Matthew 26:65-66

A true Christian accepts this same baptism of Jesus' rejection, willing to live and speak the truth even when it offends, willing at any moment to give his or her very life for even the smallest aspect of the faith. To pay the ultimate price, that is the Spirit that is on Jesus and on His saints. To the Christian, cowardice is a completely inappropriate characteristic; one that dooms the soul to Hell.[3] The thing that has always made the Gospel so supernaturally effective is the individual believer who cannot be manipulated, cannot be bought, cannot be compromised, cannot be threatened, and cannot be stopped from of the truth of the Lord Jesus Christ.

To suffer at various levels of adversity (even when it comes from those who claim to be believers) is actually a badge of honor, for in our weakness we share with Christ Jesus a strength that cannot be found by softness and easiness. Jesus suffered before us, and He overcame His afflictions perfectly; and because He made it through His baptism, we can make it through ours, for we have been baptized into Him.

> "The Spirit itself beareth witness with our spirit,
> that we are the children of God: and if children,
> then heirs; heirs of God, and joint-heirs with Christ;
> if so be that we suffer with *him,* that we may be also
> glorified together. For I reckon that the sufferings
> of this present time *are* not worthy *to be compared*
> with the glory which shall be revealed in us."
> – Romans 8:16-18

BAPTISM AND
CHURCH UNITY

There was a problem that crept into the Early Church and that caused the Apostle Paul to pen some very important words from which we can learn today.[1]

You know by now that baptism is a practice of discipleship; and in Paul's time, the saints in Corinth began to associate themselves with the ministers who had brought them the Gospel and who had baptized them. The Corinthian Christians started going around saying, "Hey, I'm Paul's disciple," "Well, I follow Apollos," "Peter is who baptized me," or "I am a disciple of Jesus." By carving out their favorite niches in the Christian community, the Early Church began to have an identity crisis—and Christian denominationalism was born.

When Paul heard about this, he was disturbed, to say the least. He had two responses for this disunified bunch. One response was to call them "carnal." In other words he was saying, "You are not in the Spirit by doing this. This is not the will of God, this is not what the Church is all about, and this is not right!"

Paul's other response was to point them away from the human factor to the ministry of Christ. He asked the Corinthians, "Was Paul crucified for you? or were ye baptized in the name of Paul?" Of course, his ashamed audience was reminded that Jesus was crucified for them and that they had been baptized in His name.

Faith Building or Wall Building?

God never intended that you be baptized into a church group or identify yourself as a follower of a great personality or with a darling doctrine. The only name, the only faith, and the only baptism God has established for the Church is in the Lord Jesus Christ. The Bible is very, very clear that there is only one Body and that Body is Christ.[2]

Paul informed the Corinthians that we are the building and the "increase" or harvest of God. So to build and to harvest for the name and glory of a specialized aspect of Christianity is carnal! There is nothing wrong with what is called "streams" of fellowship or with pooling resources together for particular efforts. After all, it is physically impossible to know and to work with every Christian saint and church. However, you and I are, first and foremost, *Christians.* Jesus is our Founder; Jesus is our Cutting Edge; and Jesus is our Leader, our Bishop, our General Superintendent who delineates what we believe and how we practice our faith.

Never be foolish enough to say, "I was born a such-and-such and I'll die a such-and-such." Your loyalty is to be in the One who has brought you into His faith and His flock, and that is exactly why you are to be baptized into His name.

THE QUESTION OF REBAPTISM

One frequently asked question which surfaces after people get a revelation of Jesus' name and of biblical baptism is, "Should I be re-baptized?" Here are some simple helping points which relate to that question.

What Does the Bible Say?

You may be wondering, "Is rebaptism even biblical?" Well, that depends.

Some people seem to regard rebaptism as being something you do every time you get in the mood for religion and want another try at turning over a new leaf. Well, if you are expecting the water to miraculously keep you from any more bouts with temptation or to be a kind of periodical bath, then you are practicing unbiblical baptism as well as bogus Christianity. Baptism is a covenantal practice which binds you to Christ Jesus. Backsliding or straying from Jesus does not make void your baptismal commitment; what it does mean is that you are in violation of your commitment, and the thing you need to do is return to your first love and first works.

However, if you regard rebaptism as being for the sake of correcting or perfecting your discipleship then you match up with the Bible; for not only did some of John the Baptist's disciples change over to disciples of Christ[1] (being encouraged by John himself), but Paul, in fact, re-baptized John's disciples.[2]

Guidelines for Rebaptism

Biblical baptism must be done in full faith; and that goes for rebaptism as well. If you are wondering if you need to be re-baptized, ask yourself the following four questions:

1. Was my first baptism carried out with the necessary, deliberate faith *on my part*?

2. Was I wrongly baptized before into a church, a denomination, a leader, or even a doctrine?

3. Is the Holy Ghost showing me that my previous baptism was somehow imperfect (lack of revelation, insincerity, doubt, a forced baptism, etc.)?

4. Is the Lord simply prompting me to get re-baptized?

Again, baptism and rebaptism are for the sake of converting to the Jesus Christ; and the Lord's definite will is that you convert to Him.

APPLICATION ANSWERS

Chapter One

A. Christians are converts of Jesus of Nazareth, the Christ or Messiah.

B. First, it indicates that Jesus is eager to contact you. His call to you is an expression of friendliness and, in fact, of love.

Second, it means that Jesus has something on His mind. He has something to say to you, He has something He wants you to do, and He has something He wants from you. You have the privilege of receiving a personal invitation to come to Him.

C. It is common courtesy to answer a person who is talking to you. You must answer Jesus.

D. God has given Christ Jesus rule over the entire universe.

E. True.

F. In order to have immortality or eternal life, you MUST become a total convert. Actually, God is enraged if you disobey, ignore, or even show reluctance to Jesus. He considers incomplete surrender to His Son as direct rebellion. On the other hand, He regards full surrender as you loving Him.

G. Never. Jesus requires complete allegiance. That means your loyalty to Him is priority over family, friends, romantic relationships, career, money, personal pursuits, dreams, wishes, and even your very life.

Chapter Two

A. Jesus. Jesus' name means "salvation," Jesus was sent for salvation, and Jesus continues to carry out salvation.

B. No, and that is the Father's design.

C. Jesus endured *a death penalty* for you, indicating that your sins separate you from God (Isaiah 59:2; Ephesians 4:17-19) and that you, as a sinner, were God's enemy (Romans 5:10; James 4:4).

D. God is incredibly merciful, because *while you were His enemy*, He made provision for you to be reconciled with Him through Jesus Christ.

E. Yes. Those who are born of God receive a "witness" or an inner knowledge of salvation by the Holy Ghost (Romans 8:16; 2 Corinthians 1:22). If you have never had this witness, read the next point carefully and then see Revelation 3:20.

F. The Bible says to repent of your sins, be baptized in Jesus' name (remember, this is conversion), and you shall receive the Holy Spirit (which comes in Jesus' name, which speaks of Jesus, and which will lead you into the truth of Jesus). *See Acts 2:38*

Chapter Three

A. Always.

B. Christians are to use Jesus' name for everything they do.

C. Never. God has made it very simple. Jesus is the only name because Jesus is the Only Begotten of the Father.

D. Jesus' name is so powerful that anyone can use it. The only qualifications you must have is that you believe in Jesus, ask with trust and humbleness, and pray for things that are right and good (i.e., You can't pray for drugs or for help to murder someone.)

   Having said that, realize that when you use Jesus' name, the Lord will begin dealing with you. Using Jesus' name is an invitation for God to come to you.

E. The Bible makes it clear that people from every tongue will call out to Him. The Scriptures are completely absent of a pronunciation rule. However your language enunciates "Jesus," is acceptable to God.

F. No. The Father only honors Jesus' name.

G. Yes! The single and exclusive name that will tap you into the power and fellowship of God's Spirit is the name of Jesus.

Chapter Four

A. Yes.

B. By going to Jesus. He reveals God.

C. God's confirmation.

D. No. Glorifying Jesus is exactly what God's Spirit does.

E. Jesus never developed into divinity. Jesus came to earth *as* God in the flesh, and He is the Eternal Word who always *was with* God and who always *has been* God.

F. No. Jesus promised that through Him you can connect with God, but Jesus never said that you would become a god.

G. Because the Baptizer *of* the Holy Ghost is still baptizing *with* the Holy Ghost. Jesus is the same source of God's Spirit yesterday, today, and forever.

Chapter Five

A. Jesus is expert in helping you with every aspect of life.

B. No, and that is the Father's design.

C. No. Prayer to any other spiritual being is considered idolatry and witchcraft. *See Exodus 20:4-5; Deuteronomy 18:11*

D. False. The principles are simple and you will never need to use but one name: Jesus.

E. That Jesus is the same true and living God known by the Old Testament kings, priests, and prophets.

Chapter Six

A. Christians are always to seek the will of God over their personal preferences. Remember Jesus' prayer, "Not my will, but thine, be done."

B. False. God often points people away from their deeply personal agendas.

C. We are to copy, emulate, imitate Jesus in thought, word, and deed—and even in Spirit.

D. False. Your baptism into Christ means that you do the things Jesus does, and Jesus does not sin.

E. (C). While growing in godliness is indeed a process, God calls us immediately to repent of our sinfulness and begin living according to His righteousness.

F. True; however, your contentment depends on your decision to have a good and obedient attitude.

Chapter Seven

A. False. The Church proclaims and enjoys salvation but Jesus is your salvation.

B. Jesus. He is the One who is responsible for putting leaders in the Church, He gives them authority or an anointing, and He even gives them messages to deliver to His people; but He, through the Spirit, is also personally involved in speaking and ministering to His people.

C. False. Jesus laid down all the principles of the faith.

D. Yes.

E. Pray for them but keep serving the Lord. Jesus is the Head of the Church and He never changes.

F. The Church is the Body of Christ. When you are baptized into Jesus, you necessarily become part of His Body.

G. The name of Jesus. Again, the Church is called the Church and Bride of Christ.

H. Your fellow believers are your family.

Chapter Eight

A. No. Science means "knowledge" and knowledge is from God and in God. True science is conscious of spiritual things and sees in nature and nature's laws evidence of an almighty Creator who remains in control of the universe.

B. False. All things are given to Christ by the Father.

C. Yes. People are institutions and institutions are people. Therefore, all activities that include people come under the jurisdiction of God and of His Christ.

D. In no way. Man has received grace because of Jesus and His priority status; man, therefore, is obligated to Christ.

E. Your answer can be either "eternal" or "everlasting." Final punishment is called "eternal damnation," "eternal fire," "everlasting burnings," "everlasting punishment," and "everlasting destruction." Final reward is referred to as "eternal life," "life eternal," "everlasting life," and "life everlasting."

F. False. Jesus has all power, and He has the keys of death and of Hell. One day He will sentence Satan to the Lake of Fire (*see Revelation 1:18; 20:10; Matthew 25:41*).

G. False. Nowhere in Scriptures are we told that God hates judgment; in fact, we find just the opposite (*see Psalms 37:28; Isaiah 61:8; Revelation 15:1-4; John 9:39*). Jesus will indeed take vengeance on the ungodly at the last day; but He would rather grant individuals mercy, which is why He died on the cross (*see Ezekiel 33:11; Micah 7:18; Ephesians 2:4-7*).

H. No. If Jesus is your Lord and Savior, you will be raised from the dead unto immortality, justified at the judgment, and live with Jesus forever.

ENDNOTES

CHAPTER ONE

[1] This is desert between Elim and Mount Sinai (Exodus 16:1; Numbers 33:11-12) and most likely the present day plain of el-Markha.

[2] 1 Corinthians 10:2

[3] Notice, too, that the children of Israel received the Law of Moses only after they became baptized.

[4] See also John 3:22, 26

[5] 1 John 5:6-11

[6] Micah 5:2

[7] Title for the Messiah

[8] Another title for the Messiah

[9] Still another title for the Messiah

[10] Chicago Manual Style (CMS): *Dictionary.com Unabridged (v 1.1)*. Random House, Inc. http://dictionary.reference.com/browse/convert (accessed: April 27, 2007).

[11] James 2:14-26

[12] This word means to hesitate; to be partial (not complete); to judge or to discriminate (as with options).

[13] Hebrews 11:6

CHAPTER TWO

[1] *Strong's Exhaustive Concordance*: Hebrew Dictionary 3444

[2] See chapters 1 and 2 of *Understanding the Difficult Words of Jesus*, 1994 Revised Edition, by David Bivin and Roy Blizzard, Jr., Destiny Image Publishers

[3] Matthew 1:21

[4] Mark 10:47

[5] Matthew 8:29

[6] Matthew 27:37

[7] For example: if you have stolen something, you will give it back. If you are in a sexual relationship outside of marriage, you will immediately break off that relationship. If you have lied, gossiped, hated, fought, etc. you will go to the other party(s) and ask forgiveness.

[8] Matthew 24:13

[9] John 14:21, 23

CHAPTER THREE

[1] John 4:1-2

[2] For example: Genesis 17:1; Exodus 6:3; 15:26; Leviticus 20:8

CHAPTER FOUR

[1] "... both Lord and Christ."

[2] 1 Timothy 3:16

[3] John 3:34

CHAPTER FIVE

[1] Hebrews 1:2

[2] John 1:1, 14

[3] *Strong's Exhaustive Concordance*, Greek dictionary, #4137

[4] John 6:37

[5] I also included the phrases "with ... in ... by ... through Christ" and " with ... in ... by ... through the Son."

[6] John 10:9

CHAPTER SIX

[1] The name of the man in this story has been changed.

[2] Luke 7:23

[3] John 8:34, 44; Romans 6:20-23; Ephesians 2:2; 1 John 3:8

[4] James 1:12; Hebrews 3:6, 14; 12:1-11; Psalms 94:12-13

[5] 1 Corinthians 10:13

CHAPTER SEVEN

[1] See 1577, *Thayer's Greek-English Lexicon of the New Testament*

[2] The candlesticks are symbolic of individual assemblies. See Revelation 1:10-20

[3] Deuteronomy 31:29 Also verses 21 and 27.

[4] 2 Peter 1:4

CHAPTER EIGHT

[1] Genesis 1:26; Psalms 8:4-6

[2] The Greek word *douleuo* is used 27 times in the New Testament and is mostly translated as "to serve;" however, its literal translation is "to be a slave."

EPILOGUE

[1] Ecclesiastes 7:8

APPENDIX ONE

[1] 1 Timothy 4:5

[2] For example: Acts 8:36-37; 16:31; 18:8; Romans 10:9; Hebrews 11:6; 1 John 5:4

[3] Colossians 2:11

APPENDIX TWO

[1] Luke 23:43

[2] Luke 24:47; Acts 2:38; 10:43

[3] Matthew 3:5-6

[4] Acts 22:16

APPENDIX THREE

[1] See original text, Canons 1 and 7 of the First Council of Constantinople.

[2] The word used is translaed "anathema."

[3] Mark 16:20

[4] Ephesians 2:20

[5] Ecclesiastes 7:8

APPENDIX FIVE

[1] Matthew 20:22-23; Mark 10:38-39

[2] Luke 12:50

[3] Revelation 21:8; Mark 8:38; John 12:25; Luke 12:4-5

APPENDIX SIX

[1] 1 Corinthians 1:11-17; 3:1-11

[2] Romans 12:4-5; 1 Corinthians 12:12-13

APPENDIX SEVEN

[1] Acts 18:24-28; John 1:35-37, 40; 3:26-36; 10:40-41

[2] Acts 19:1-7

NOTES

NOTES

NOTES

NOTES

NOTES

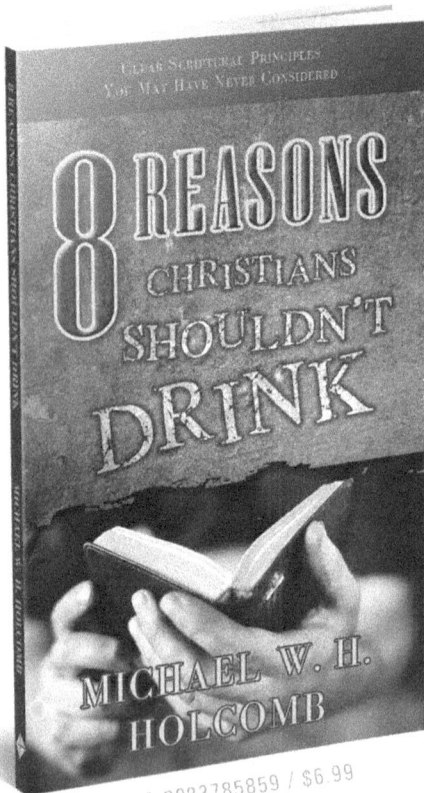

THE BOOK THAT DARES TO CONFRONT AN ENTRENCHED BUT UNSCRIPTURAL TRADITION

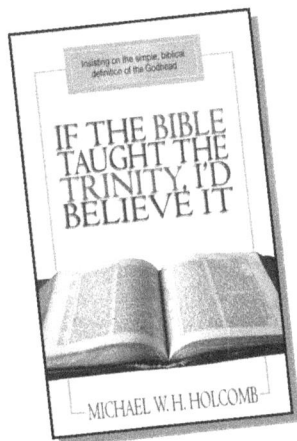

IF THE BIBLE TAUGHT THE TRINITY, I'D BELIEVE IT

This book will bring you closer to God because it tells you the truth about God.

What you will discover

- Reliable references that the Trinity is not in the Bible
- History of how the Trinity evolved
- Problems caused by the Trinity doctrine
- The scriptural mystery of the Godhead

AVAILABLE IN PAPERBACK OR EBOOK!

www.bibledays.org
www.amazon.com
www.bn.com

CHECK US OUT AT

BIBLEDAYS.ORG

Downloadable audio sermons

More BDM books

Podcasts[†]

Email:
contact@bibledays.org

Write:
BibleDays Ministries
PO Box 2515
Williamsport, PA 17703

[†] Launching March 17, 2014